Oda Nobunaga: The Battle of Okehazama

How Japan's Fiercest Warlord Began the Unification of Japan

By Les Paterson

Published by Jetlag Press (http://www.jetlagpress.com)

Cover image: "Night Rain at Narumi" by Kuniyoshi

Cover Design by Christopher West and Brent Massey

For information about special discounts for bulk purchases, please contact orders@jetlagpress.com

---

Paterson, Les
    Oda Nobunaga: The Battle of Okehazama

    1. Japanese History. 2. Japanese Samurai. I. Title.
    ISBN 978-0-9790397-4-4

Printed in the USA and UK

Dedication

To Chrissie Jr.

Owari no Utsuke de owaru ka. Tenka wo toru ka.

Contents

Timeline and Maps

Oda Nobunaga Timeline

1534 Oda Nobunaga was born at Nagoya Castle, Owari Province. Birth name Kichibōshi.

1542 First battle of Azukisaka pitted against the Imagawa.

1546 Nobunaga's genpuku held at Furuwatari Castle. Name changed to Oda Saburō Nobunaga.

1547 Nobunaga receives his first baptism of fire at the battle Mikawa Kira Ōhama against the Imagawa.

1548 Nobunaga marries Saitō Dōsan's daughter Nōhime. Nobuhide defeated at the Second Battle of Azukisaka.

1549 Oda Nobuhide loses Anjō Castle. Oda Nobuhiro captured.

1551 Oda Nobuhide passes away.

1553 Hirate Masahide commits suicide. Nobunaga meets his father-in-law, Saitō Dōsan at Shōtokuji Temple.

1554 Nobunaga defeats the Imagawa at the Battle of Muraki. Name changed to Oda Kazusa no Suke Nobunaga.

1555 Nobunaga moves to Kiyosu Castle.

1556 Saitō Dōsan killed by his son Yoshitatsu resulting in the break up of the Saitō-Oda alliance. Nobunaga's younger brother, Nobuyuki revolts and defeated at the Battle of Inō.

1557 Nobuyuki revolts again and killed by Nobunaga.

1558 Nobunaga attacks Iwakura's Oda Nobukata at the Battle of Ukino. Tokugawa Ieyasu receives his first baptism of fire at the Battle of Terabe. Battle of Shinano pitted against Matsudaira Ietsugu.

1559 Nobunaga makes his first trip to Kyoto. Iwakura Castle attacked and destroyed resulting in the unification of Owari.

1560 The prelude to the Battle of Okehazama: Battle of Mikawa Kira pitted against the Imagawa in Mikawa. Battle of Okehazama: Nobunaga defeats Imagawa Yoshimoto.

Imagawa Yoshimoto Timeline

1519 Born and named Hōgikumaru.

1522 Hōgikumaru enters Zentokuji.

1526 Imagawa Yoshichika, Yoshimoto's father dies.

1532 Name changed to Sengakushōhō.

1536 Battle of Hanakura, defeats Genkōetan. Yoshimoto's older brother, Ujiteru dies.
Name changed to Yoshimoto; character "Yoshi" coming from the 12ᵗʰ Ashikaga shogun Yoshiharu.

1537 Yoshimoto marries Takeda Nobutora's daughter.

1538 Yoshimoto's son, Ujizane is born.

1541 Takeda Harunobu (Shingen) banishes his father, Nobutora. Yoshimoto allows Nobutora sanctuary in Sunpu.

1546 The Imagawa attacks the Toda family at Imabashi Castle (Yoshida Castle).

1547 Yoshimoto attacks Tahara Castle occupied by Toda Norimitsu.

1550 Yoshimoto's wife, Jukeiin passes away.

1552 Yoshimoto's daughter marries Takeda Shingen's son, Yoshinobu.

1553 *Kana Mokuroku Tsuika* completed.

1554 Hōjō, Takeda, and Imagawa alliance completed at Zentokuji.

1555 Taigen Sūfu passes away.

1557 Yoshimoto bequeaths the clan to his son Ujizane.

1560 Yoshimoto's attempted march to Kyoto fails, killed at the Battle of Okehazama.

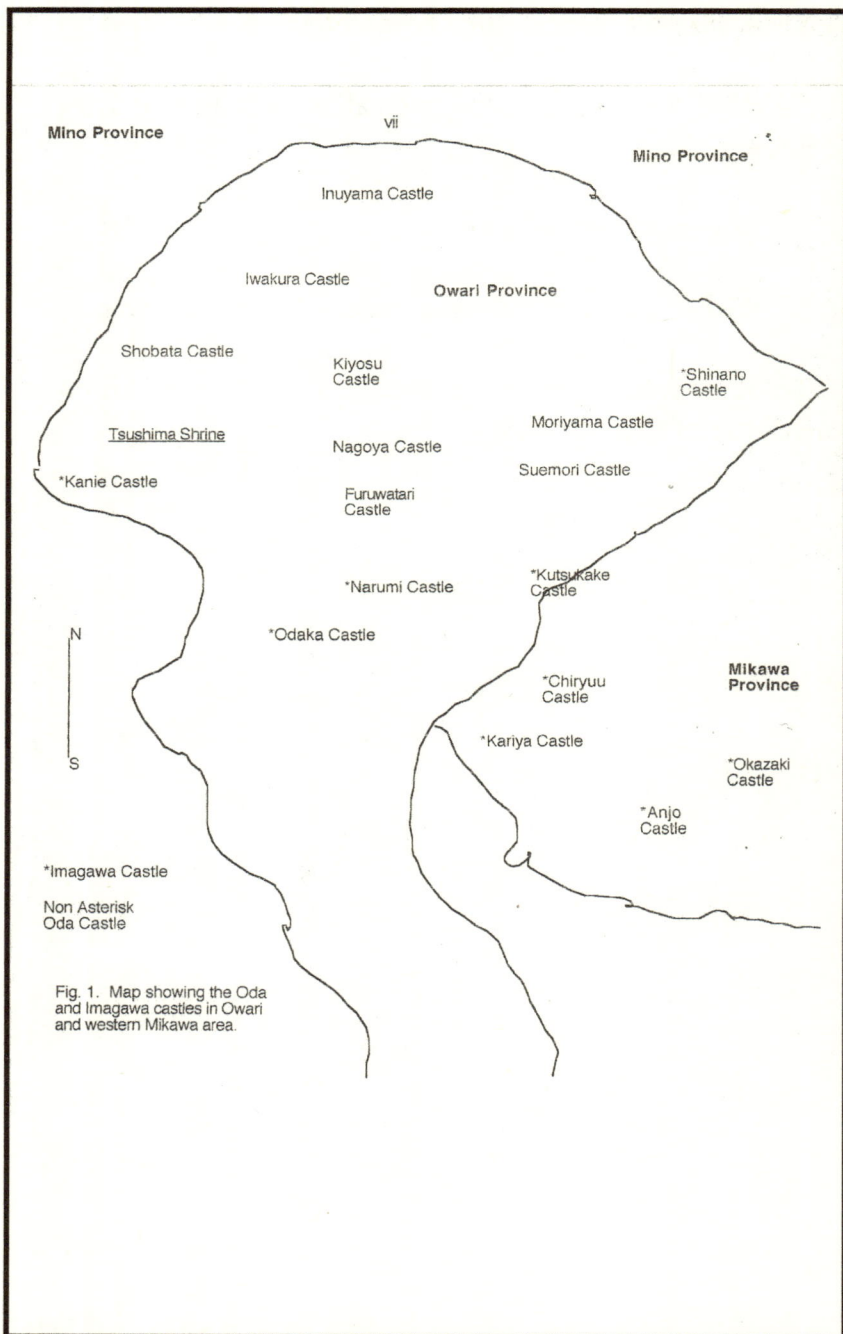

Mino Province

vii

Mino Province

Inuyama Castle

Iwakura Castle

Owari Province

Shobata Castle

Kiyosu
Castle

*Shinano
Castle

Tsushima Shrine

Moriyama Castle

Nagoya Castle

*Kanie Castle

Suemori Castle

Furuwatari
Castle

*Narumi Castle

*Kutsukake
Castle

N

*Odaka Castle

**Mikawa
Province**

*Chiryuu
Castle

*Kariya Castle

S

*Okazaki
Castle

*Anjo
Castle

*Imagawa Castle

Non Asterisk
Oda Castle

Fig. 1. Map showing the Oda
and Imagawa castles in Owari
and western Mikawa area.

viii

From Atsuta
Shrine

N

S

Ise
Bay

Tenpaku
River

Fort
Tange

Other Route

Narumi
Castle

Fort Zenshouji

Ogi River

Fort Nakajima

Shinchoo-Koo ki
Route

Imagawa
Army

Fort Washizu

Odaka
Castle

Fort Marune

Yoshimoto's
Main Army

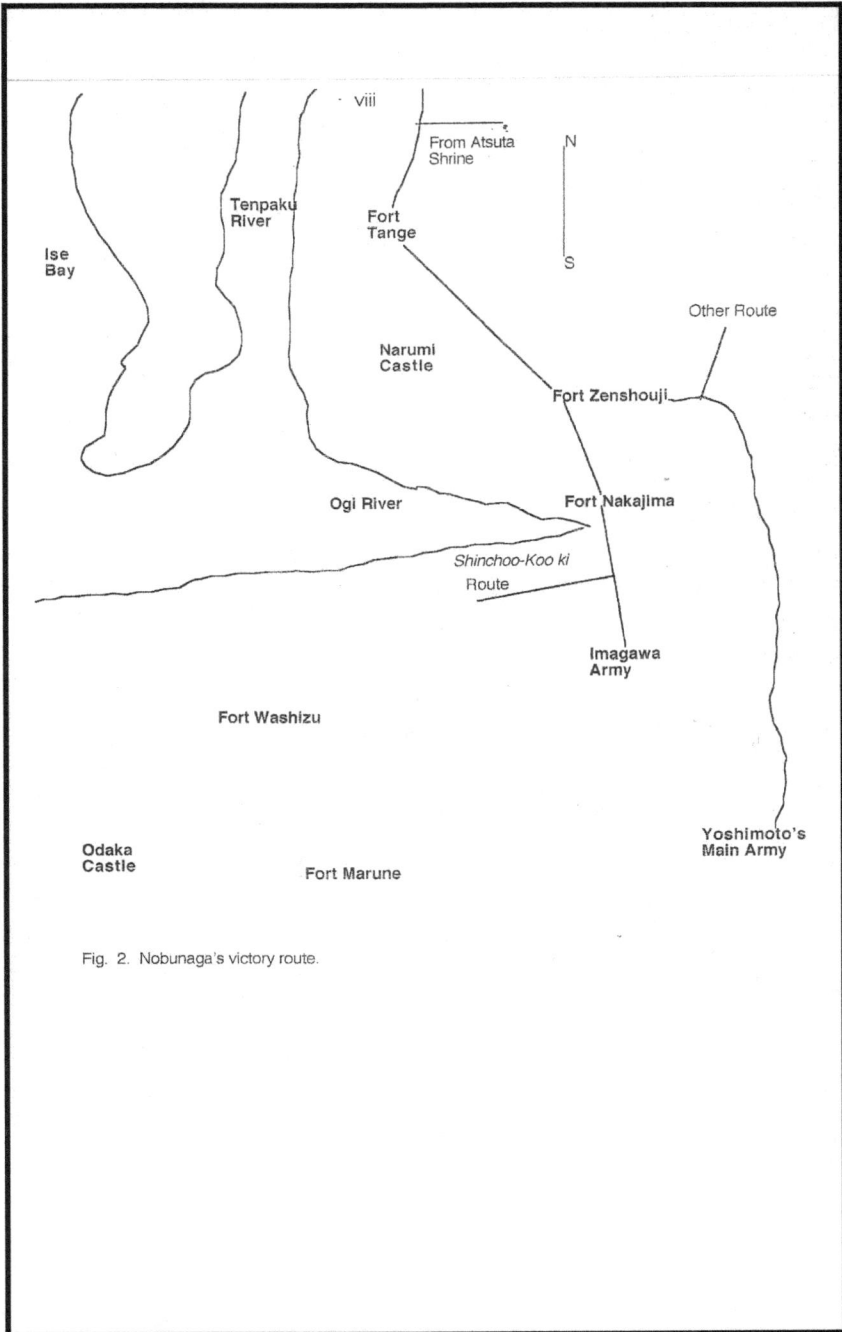

Fig. 2. Nobunaga's victory route.

ix

Fort   Mizuno
Tange Tatewaki

Aihara

Tenpaku
River

Ise
Bay

Narumi   Fort   Sakuma
Castle   Zenshouji   Nobumori
Okabe
Motonobu

Ogi River

Fort   Kajikawa
Nakajima Takahide

Fort   Oda Genba
Washizu

Odaka   Tokugawa
Castle   Ieyasu
Udono Nagateru

Fort
Marune
Sakuma Daigaku

Okehazama

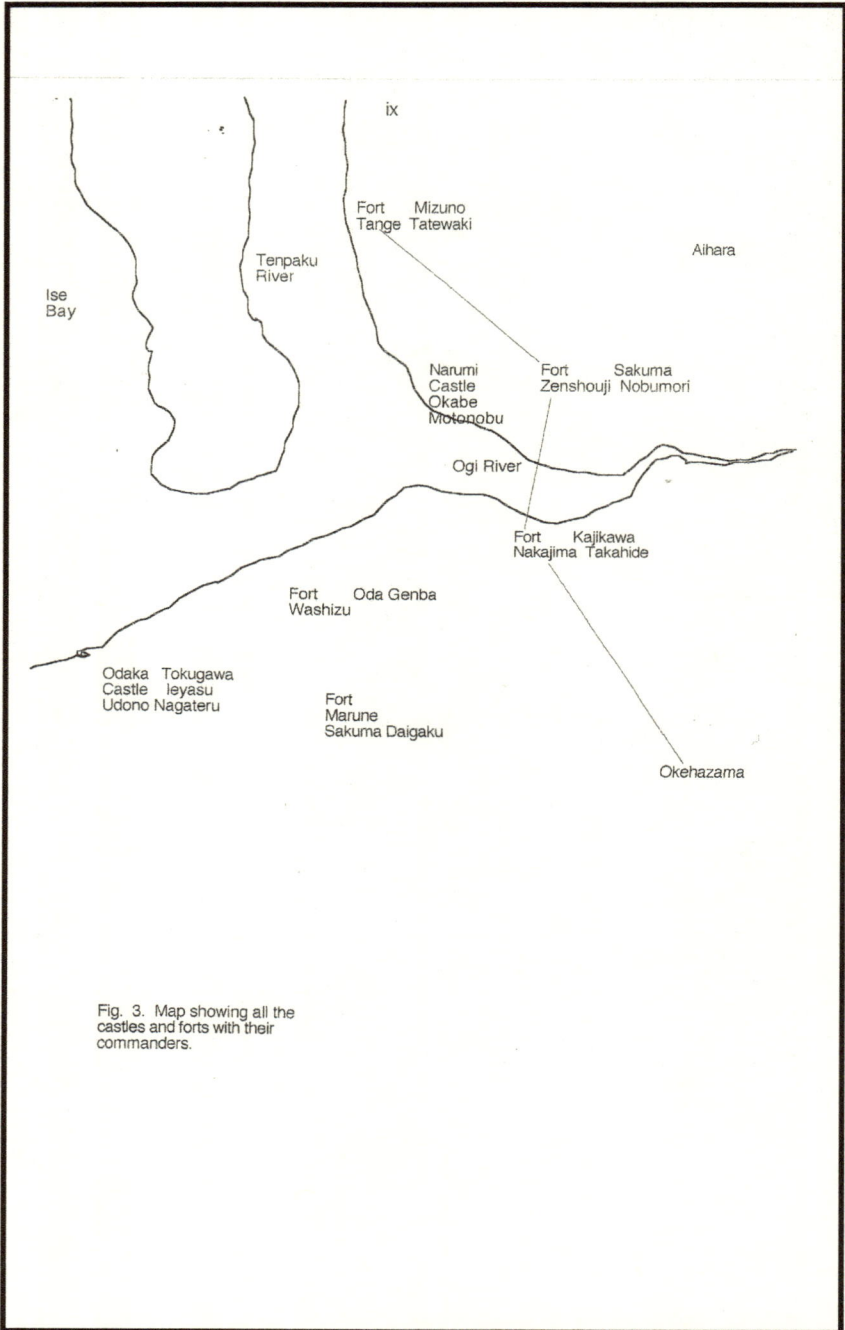

Fig. 3. Map showing all the
castles and forts with their
commanders.

INTRODUCTION

THE Battle of Okehazama is one of those unexplained events. It was one of the most significant battles in Japanese military history. How did Oda Nobunaga, a man who was supposed to be a complete idiot defeat a much more powerful warlord? Twenty-five thousand soldiers marching to Kyoto and was defeated by an army of 3,000. Okehazama was the Japanese version of David and Goliath. This book will have several sections which will explain Nobunaga's unification of the Oda clan, the wars against the Imagawa family, and the death of Imagawa Yoshimoto.

There were many reasons why the author decided to write a book about the Battle of Okehazama. The author was continually frustrated with English sources related to Oda Nobunaga and the Sengoku Era. Many were not descriptive enough and were too general. Furthermore, countless books did not include a bibliography. This book will give the reader a descriptive account as well as a bibliography that a scholar can use for future reference.

Oda Nobunaga's early life made clear because it will have a lot to do with his tactics dealing with Imagawa Yoshimoto at Okehazama. Nobunaga's use of firearms was important. His dealing with his father-in-law Saitō Dōsan in 1553 at Shōtokuji was so bizarre it helped him in the end. Nobunaga's youth was not the typical Sengoku warlord. He often liked to play with his friends and his character was nothing like other samurai. He was a rare man of the times and his days as a young lad helps the reader to understand Okehazama.

The Battle of Muraki in 1554 was an engagement between Nobunaga and the Imagawa army. It was the prelude to come six years later. The battle itself was intense and it was an all day affair. Nobunaga will lose many soldiers; however, it will give him a taste of what was to come. Muraki additionally gave Nobunaga needed confidence that he needed to not only fight the Imagawa, but also to control his Owari domain as well. Last, was the faith he received at Muraki from Saitō Dōsan. Part of the Muraki victory was due to Dōsan's support for his son-in-law.

Okehazama, the battle itself, was a brilliant plan of a desperate sneak attack. Nobunaga had no other choice but to attack Imagawa Yoshimoto. His use of intelligence, leadership, and character would change Sengoku warfare forever. Okehazama quickly changed warfare from military exploitation to the age of intelligence.

Post Okehazama included the independence of Matsudaira Motoyasu (Tokugawa Ieyasu). The alliance between Oda Nobunaga and Tokugawa Ieyasu, which lasted almost twenty years, was a rarity in Sengoku Japan, and the fall of the Imagawa clan and their role in Japan. It was the fool who liberated Ieyasu from Yoshimoto, who was harsh on Ieyasu and the men of Mikawa. To the reader, the explanation of the problems between Nobunaga and Ieyasu will have nothing to do with the battle itself, but it has a lot to do with it. Okehazama was the result for both parties. Without Okehazama, the two men would not have accomplished the goal of unifying war torn Japan.

The conclusion will defend the function of top-quality use of intelligence and strong leadership in the modern world. It will also explain how Okehazama can help with the war on terror. Okehazama will further justify the rise of a new unifier and leader of Sengoku Japan: Oda Nobunaga.

Core sources that will be used are the following: Stephen Turnbull, *Battles of the Samurai.*, Owada Tetsuo, *Rekishi Documento: Okehazama no Tatakai.*, A.L. Sadler, *The Maker of Modern Japan.*, Ōta Gyūichi, *Shinchō-Kō ki.*, Jeroen Lamers, *Japonius Tyrannus.*, and Neil McMullin, *Buddhism and the State in Sixteenth-Century Japan.*

Owada Tetsuo's *Okehazama no Tatakai* is recent and is a highly valuable resource. The book has both the Oda and Imagawa family lines as well as who was killed in action during the battle. More important, it highlighted Nobunaga's use of intelligence. The book is opinionated and one of the best covering the conflict. His work on the subject was skillfully researched and written.

The *Shinchō-Kō ki* written by Ōta Gyūichi (1527-1613?) is the biography of Oda Nobunaga. Gyūichi actually served under Nobunaga as an ashigaru (foot soldier). He was skilled with the bow and came from Nobunaga's Owari domain. Highly useful, but sometimes propagandizes Nobunaga's victories.   As for Okehazama, Gyūichi described it appropriately and the possibilities of him participating in the battle were extremely high.

Oze Hoan, who wrote the *Shinchōki*, is another biography of Oda Nobunaga. As for Okehazama, he was born four years after the battle (1564-1640). He likewise wrote the *Taikōki*, the biography of Toyotomi Hideyoshi.

Lamers's book is recently new, modern, and brings a new perspective on the career of Oda Nobunaga. However, he did not do a good job and an injustice on describing the Battle of Okehazama with only a few sentences. What he failed to realized Okehazama was one of the key events that jump-started Nobunaga's career. In spite of everything, as for Nobunaga's family and their history, a major achievement.

Buddhism and the State in Sixteenth-Century Japan explained Nobunaga's ten-year war against the Ishiyama Honganji and the massacre of Mt. Hiei in 1571. The description on Nobunaga's personality was excellent. Even though it did not describe Okehazama in detail, it provided extensive information on Nobunaga's character, which was historic. Character was one of Nobunaga's first-class assets and it helped him at Okehazama.

Sadler's book, *The Maker of Modern Japan*, has stood up through the times. Written in the 1930s, it depicted Tokugawa Ieyasu's career. His work illustrated the other side of the story. It centered on the relationship between Ieyasu and Yoshimoto. Sadler took great care to illustrate Yoshimoto's mishaps. Sadler's beautiful work of art has stood up to the test of time.

Turnbull's book, *The Battles of the Samurai*, was above average at best. Even though it was above average; thus, it was still a decent reference book. The main problem: the book was too general. When interpreting the Battle of Okehazama he did not go deep enough. He did provide the reader with enough information to illustrate what happened during the clash. Overall the book was useful considering it was written in English and his sources were sufficient.

Another source is the *Mikawa Monogatari* written by Ōkubo Hikozaemon, a retainer of Tokugawa Ieyasu. The *Mikawa Monogatari* explained the Matsudaira clan and Ieyasu's history. It explained the two battles where Oda Nobuhide and the Imagawa army fought at Azuki-kura in the 1540s. Furthermore, the *Mikawa Monogatari* also illustrated the other side of the Battle of Okehazama. The only problem with Ōkubo was he was born the same year the battle took place (1560).

Why is the Battle of Okehazama important? Why was the battle a significant part in Japanese military history? The answer lies on the border between the two clans and the use of human intelligence. The *Oda Nobunaga no Subete ga Wakaru Hon* described it as a boundary battle between rival warlords.[1] For instance, Nobunaga occupied Owari while Yoshimoto held Mikawa with the help of hostage Matsudaira Motoyasu (Tokugawa Ieyasu, the name in use in this book), the border province of Owari. Border wars were common during the Sengoku Era (Warring States). For example, battles between Uesugi Kenshin-Takeda Shingen at Kawanakajima, Tokugawa Ieyasu-Shingen again at Mikatagahara, and Oda Nobuhide-Saitō Dōsan at Inabayama were all border wars.   Historically, Okehazama proved to be Nobunaga's finest hour.

1

Words from Hell

I have, after twelve years of fighting, succeeded in taking the whole province of Owari. Yoshimoto has opposed me continually all this time, but as yet I have never had any reason to fear him. And now am I quietly to submit to his rule without striking a blow? Would this be maintaining the reputation of my family for brave deeds? Would this be soldier-like conduct? No, rather than do this, I will shave my head and become a priest. To make plans for submission with nothing but report to guide us-whoever heard such cowardice? Should Yoshimoto come, we will give him a warm reception on the borders-we will fight to the death rather than allow him to pass through our province.[2]

Oda Nobunaga, the man, the myth, and the legend was born in 1534 in the province of Owari, near Nagoya. Nobunaga was born at Nagoya Castle. Others historians he was born at Shobata Castle in Owari.[3] His mother, Dota Gozen was from the Dota family (daughter of Dota Masahisa of Kani-bu of Mino).[4] She would additionally give birth to Nobunaga's rival brother, Nobuyuki.

This man would devote his entire life trying to unify Japan under his rule (under his slogan: Tenka Fubu). He is famously known for the new advances in military tactics such as firearms, development of the ashigaru, iron clad ships, strong leadership, a capitalist, free trader, and a mind to hire great military generals. He was a "Soldier of Fortune" (fūunji) from the day he was born until he died tragically in 1582.

From *Sources of Japanese Tradition*:

His ambition, which he narrowly failed to achieve, was 'to bring the whole country under one sword' (tenka-fubu), a motto inscribed on his personal seal. His qualifications for this stupendous task were somewhat paradoxical: a single minded, ruthless determination to attain his ends, coupled with an amazing flexibility and open-mindedness as to means.[5]

Raised Nobunaga was in the period known as "Sengoku Jidai" an era in Japan where the sword was mightier than the pen. Bloodshed was king!

Origins of the Oda Clan and Nobunaga's Early Life

The Oda clan can be traced back to the domain Oda no Shō in present day Fukui Prefecture (Echizen Province), according to Nobunaga's modern biographer, Jeroen Lamers.[6] They were the managers and priests of the Oda Tsurugi Shrine and the family name came from the geographic area.[7] Beginning in the fifteenth century, the Oda moved to Owari, which the clan settled and made their presence known.[8]

Nobunaga was the third son of Oda Nobuhide, who was one of the three-deputy shugo (shugodai) of the Shiba family, the hereditary shugo of Owari Province, and a senior in one of the two bands that were competing for control of Owari.[9] As for Nobuhide, it noted in the *Shinchō-Kō ki*, that he was wise man and made many allies.[10] He also gave funds to repair the Imperial Palace in Kyoto. Before his death in 1551, he was a key individual in Owari and recognized at the Imperial Court in Kyoto. Nobuhide throughout the 1540s to 1550s took over the Mikawa villages governed by the Matsudaira clan.[11] Soon the Matsudaira family pledged their allegiance to the Imagawa for help against the Oda. In return, the Matsudaira sent their heir to Suruga as a hostage. However, the Oda captured the young lad. Nobuhide kept the young lad famously known as Tokugawa Ieyasu.[12]

Nobunaga's behavior and his days as a youth are well worth noting. It was said when he was a baby, he had the habit of biting off the teat of his wet nurse, and it was necessary to change his wet nurse often.[13] When he was about the age of thirteen years of age he applied himself to swimming and horsemanship, and at the same time, he participated in mock battles with wooden spears everyday with other boys.[14] During his childhood, he fell in love with new weapon from Europe: guns, and quickly became fond of them. In fact, after his marriage to Nōhime, he placed an order of 500 matchlock guns from Kunitomo gun factory.[15] Already at a young age, he saw the future of warfare in Sengoku Japan.

His childhood was similar to any youth who lived in the countryside. One day while playing in the garden, he picked up a poisonous snake. He brought the serpent home to show his family. However, his family and retainers were in complete shock and shame.[16] For Nobunaga, he was having a good time being a young country boy.

He wore a short-sleeved shirt and a bag of flints hung from his waist. His hair done in chasen style, attached with red and green cords, and a long sword in a lacquered casing hung from his waist.[17] Sugawara replies on Nobunaga's youth, "He cut such an odd figure that others called him a fool behind his back."[18] As McMullin continues, "He strode around town laden with chestnuts, persimmons, and melons, and with his mouth stuffed with rice cakes."[19] His often loose, unrestrained, and zany childhood helped him prepare for the future. The masses often mocked Nobunaga because he was a freethinker. An individualist was a threat to traditional society.

Before his genpuku and first taste of battle, Nobunaga who was still a young boy received Nagoya Castle.[20] Nobuhide bequeathed it because he constructed Furuwatari Castle, which was near Atsuta Shrine.[21] The act accomplished was around 1542 or before. Nobuhide was thinking ahead for the future. He did not know that young Nobunaga would have the same qualities as his father such as intelligence, leadership, and a brain that was far ahead of anybody else.

Nobunaga at the age of thirteen had his genpuku or the ritual of manhood at Furuwatari Castle in 1546.[22] His name changed from Kichibōshi to Oda Saburō Nobunaga. The name

Saburō would stick around until 1554 when it became Oda Kazusa no Suke Nobunaga. Many of his father's retainers including Hirate Masahide were there to praise him. A lush banquet prepared by the family was to honor young Nobunaga. A year later, he received his first taste of action at the Battle of Kira Ōhama in Mikawa and the opponent-the Imagawa!

The battle was not beyond burning some places here and there. Nobunaga was on a horse wearing armor, haori, and a crimson hood. His father's retainer Hirate Masahide also assisted him. The following day he returned to Nagoya along with rest of the Oda army.[23] That day Nobunaga proved his worth. He had nerves of steel and never showed any signs of panic.

Nobunaga was eighteen years of age his father Nobuhide died in 1551.[24] His father's death was important whereas it will clarify Nobunaga's unpredictable behavior and character. During Nobuhide's funeral, Nobunaga threw powdered incense at the altar. He did not even bow in respect of his deceased father. Sugawara stated, "His behavior at the funeral reinforced his reputation as a fool."[25] There is evidence why Nobunaga played the role of the "fool" because it was the only way to survive. The role (fool) offered no direct threat to older and more powerful members of the Oda family who were competing for control of Nobuhide's domain.[26]

Not everyone called Nobunaga a fool. During the funeral procession, a traveling monk from Kyushu saw the fool's true character. The monk replied, "That person will become a powerful warlord in the future!"[27] The monk discovered the freethinking attitude of Nobunaga. To the monk's opinion, a maverick was a wise man. Soon after Nobuhide's death, Nobunaga was quickly involved in a power struggle with his relatives over the Owari domain.

Luís Fróis, the Portuguese Jesuit missionary, has an explanation on Nobunaga's attitude about his father's funeral. He would have more contact with Nobunaga than any other foreigner would during the Sengoku Era. He knew the idiot well and quickly became friends. His theory was the Buddhist monks were responsible for Nobuhide's death. One must caution Fróis considering he was from Europe and his judgment of them were hardly positive at all. Fróis illustrated:

When his father lay mortally ill in Owari, Nobunaga asked the bonzes to pray for his life and asked them whether he would recover from his illness. They assured him that he would, but died a few days later. Nobunaga then had the bonzes thrown into a temple with the doors locked from the outside; he told the bonzes that, as they lied to him about the health of his father, they had better pray to their idols with greater devotion for their own lives. After surrounding them on the outside, he shot some of them to death with harquebuses.[28]

An Oda retainer (Hirate Masahide) in response of Nobunaga's outrage behavior disemboweled himself to disapprove of his actions. Masahide's death would be a major blow to him. He was in complete shock! Though Nobunaga might have felt Masahide was an old man, yet he did admire his wisdom. One day Nobunaga was hawking (takagari) and threw a piece of meat, and the hawk caught in the air. Then he said in tears, "Masahide, eat what I just caught!"[29]   After the death of Masahide, Nobunaga knew he must change his attitude if he wanted to stay in power. The fool would still be a freethinking maverick, but a mature one.

Nobunaga did regret Masahide's death, but in no way it changed his attitude towards religion. In addition to the loss, he built Seishūji Temple in honor of Masahide. Hirate Masahide was a refined man in the arts, and known to be fond of tea, and linked haiku.[30] Nobunaga was the opposite, and often played around with his friends or practiced the art of war by himself. He would rather be his own than a man bound by traditional authority. As for the temple's abbot, he placed a man named Takugen Shūon to run the place of worship. Takugen recommended Nobunaga to rename Inoguchi to Gifu in 1567.

He did change his ways, but as for religion throughout his lifetime, he never believed in Shintō or Buddhist deities.[31]   This was one the many reasons why he battled against the Ikkō sect and religious militants for so long in his military career.

Before Nobuhide passed away, he approved a proposal that his son to wed Kichō no Kata or more famously known as Nōhime in 1548, who was around fourteen years of age at the time, and was the daughter of Saitō Dōsan.[32] Dōsan's nickname was the Viper of Mino. He was an oil merchant who turned warrior and was successful in resisting the Oda and Toki clans.[33] The person who would help set up the marriage and the alliance was Hirate Masahide. According to the *Mino no kuni shokyū-ki*, Nobunaga and Nōhime were married on February 24, 1549.[34] As for Nobunaga and his relationship with women, he was known to be a playboy, and had several beautiful concubines. It was due in part of his physique. He was an attractive man that Japanese beauties adored.

The reason why Nobuhide wanted his son to marry Dōsan's daughter was to conclude a treaty among the two clans.[35] Arranged marriages between rival samurai families were widespread during this time. Paul Varley explained:

...,daimyos tended to use their own sisters, daughters and nieces--often in the most heartless fashion--as marriage pawns in their political and military maneuvering with rival chieftains of other domains.[36]

The marriage was vital for the Oda clan. Dōsan had trounced Nobuhide throughout the 1540s. With his son wed to Dōsan's daughter, Nobuhide's job was a little easier. He could concentrate against the Imagawa if he wanted to. For Dōsan, marrying off his daughter was a good idea whereas Nobunaga was still an idiot then, according to the masses. Dōsan thought he could take advantage of the fool later on in the future. Instead, it was the complete opposite.

Nōhime's mother, Ōmi no Kata, was Akechi Mitsutsugu's daughter. Oddly enough, it was Nōhime's cousin, Akechi Mitsuhide, who would later take her husband's life.[37] Ōmi no Kata did not live long after her daughter's marriage to Nobunaga. She passed away at the age of thirty-nine in 1551.

Nōhime was an intriguing and lovely woman. She was born in 1535 at Sagiyama Castle (Gifu City). Unfortunately, there is not enough information about her. She was intelligent, strong willed, and a woman with nerves of steel. Nōhime's name changed to Azuchi-dono later in life. Sadly, Nōhime never had any children and it was highly possible she was barren. Her date of her death was 9 July 1612 at the age of seventy-eight. Nōhime's grave is at Sōkenin, a subtemple of Daitokuji in Kyoto. That same year, Onabe no Kata, one of Nobunaga's beautiful concubines, also passed away.

One famous account was between Dōsan and his daughter just before the marriage. Dōsan gave Nōhime a dagger to kill her new husband if he was indeed a fool. However, Nōhime told her father she might have to use the dagger against him. Dōsan laughed! He reminded her she was truly the Viper's daughter.

Nōhime would later be a spy for her father. Why was she a spy? Dōsan might have had some uneasy feelings about his son-in-law. Of course, Nōhime did what her father told her to do. The story goes that the fool would slip out of bed every night for several hours. This puzzled her. She asked why he was doing this. Nobunaga replied that he made an agreement with two of her father's retainers to help overthrow the Saitō. Nobunaga would be on night watch to look out for a fire signal. In the evening, the signal seen and it would give the perfect opportunity to assassinate his father-in-law.

Nōhime reported to her father about the plan. Dōsan killed the two men who were plotting against him, but reality proved it was a lie! Nobunaga did this on purpose to weaken Dōsan's Mino domain without knowing it was false. It was an ideal plan for Nobunaga. It further proved how chilling and cunning his schemes could be.

The Meeting at Shōtokuji Temple

The meeting between Nobunaga and Dōsan has to be illustrated. There were four reasons why the meeting took place. (1) Dōsan never met Nobunaga, (2) to see if Nobunaga was a fool, (3) to find out if Owari was weak enough to invade, and (4) to see if the alliance was good enough to continue. Dōsan was supposed to teach his son-in-law a lesson. However, it was the other way around.

The meeting took place in 1553 at Shōtokuji in Tonda near the Mino-Owari border. The temple was a representative of the Honganji located in Osaka (modern day Osaka Castle). Dōsan wanted to know the truth about his new son-in-law. He secretly spied on Nobunaga in a shack while the Oda troops were marching along.[38] To the surprise of Dōsan, his son-in-law brought a legion that would terrify him. Nobunaga's troops had long crimson spears and a force of five hundred men with matchlock rifles.[39] Dōsan was stunned! Guns were still new to Japan and Nobunaga swiftly adapted to them with ease.

Infamous was his attire. His kimono had one sleeve down; sword scabbard lovely decorated, and had seven or eight more things with him in his tiger/leopard skin short hakama. He wore a hemp bracelet (used for guns) and a rope cord used as a sash.[40] *Rekishi Gunzō* "Gekishin Oda Nobunaga" has a replica color picture what Nobunaga might have worn that day before meeting his father-in-law and after changing in proper attire.[41] Dōsan had to be in great shock! His son-in-law embarrassed him, but more was to come.

At the temple, Nobunaga changed into proper clothes. While he was waiting for his father-in-law, he had other ideas. Two of Dōsan's retainers showed him the way to the room. Nobunaga just leaned against a pillar as if nothing special has happened. Then Hotta Dōkū introduced Dōsan to the fool, and Nobunaga replied, "Is that so!"[42] Dōsan's head had to be spinning! His son-in-law was in rags and now dressed as an aristocrat. Nobunaga was clearly enjoying the moment.

A Saitō retainer named Kasuga Tango gave Nobunaga some rice gruel to eat. Both Nobunaga and Dōsan exchanged cups of sake. With the food tasteless, Nobunaga stood up and left. Dōsan would send off his son-in-law, but with a heavy heart. He had to feel awful. The men of Mino (Saitō) had shorter spears than the Oda and their confidence was broken. A retainer of the Saitō came to Dōsan to ask him about the meeting. Dōsan replied, "I feel regrettable that my children will follow that idiot!"[43]

Nobunaga won the battle without fighting on the battlefield. He won by intimidating his father-in-law thanks to showing off his new weapons. Matchlock rifles and long spears were the key. The Mino soldiers had to be horrified. It was another great chance to display his new arsenal. He was never afraid of his fellow superiors. His superiors were obstacles who tried to prevent him from being a great warlord. For Nobunaga, his seniors were his subordinates.

The meeting with his father-in-law proved he would not tolerate haughty behavior from his seniors. Dōsan must have felt threaten that his son-in-law was a freethinker who did not recognize traditional authority. There were two key points he learned from the meeting: Nobunaga was no dupe and the Saitō-Oda alliance was adequate to continue. Dōsan did have new respect for Nobunaga. Respect because he was smart enough to recognize his son-in-law was rare and can survive in a hellish Sengoku Japan. Unfortunately, three years later Dōsan would perish by his rebellious son Yoshitatsu at the Battle of Nagaragawa. Before his death, Dōsan gave the deed of the Mino domain to Nobunaga to confirm he was the warlord of the future in Sengoku Japan.

Unification of Owari and the Oda House

Nobunaga's original headquarters was Nagoya Castle; however, he moved his base to Kiyosu in April 1555. The move to Kiyosu meant he was beginning to unite the Oda clan and the other members who oppose him eradicated. His uncle, Nobumitsu would move to Nagoya Castle in an exchange.[44] He would actually do the work for Nobunaga in occupying the Kiyosu citadel. For instance, he made a plan to pretend that he would honor the men who held Kiyosu.[45] The plan would work as the men fled. A man named Sakai Daizen somehow knew the end was near, so he fled to seek refuge at Imagawa Yoshimoto's base in Sunpu.[46]

One individual was not so lucky. Oda Nobutomo committed suicide and soon Nobunaga would occupy Kiyosu.[47] As for his uncle Nobumistu, he did not enjoy the victory treasure for long. Daizen later returned and killed Nobumitsu. Daizen and Nobunaga did not get along with each other. The reason why was the "Fool of Owari" always defeated and embarrassed Daizen.

It was meaningful for Nobunaga to acquire Kiyosu. It meant he was serious in uniting the Oda clan and getting rid of those who oppose him. If he was going to conquer Mino, he was just a little closer. Even though he still had a relationship with Dōsan; however, the situation was about to erupt into chaos for the Saitō. In 1556 Dōsan would be murdered by his son; thus, throwing out the Saitō-Oda alliance.

One of Nobunaga's disturbing times was his murder of his brother Nobuyuki. The situation he was in was not a beautiful one. There was suspicion and envy he had of Nobuyuki. Worse yet, the Oda vassals, and especially his mother held high esteem and praise of Nobuyuki.[48] This was something Nobunaga desired. There was only room for one in the Oda clan and Nobunaga made it clear he was the chosen one. There was a planned plot to revolt against the fool with the help of some Oda vassals that included Shibata Katsuie, but he soon found out the scheme and took care of it.

He was very aware of a second attempt by Nobuyuki and wanted to take care of this personal matter as soon as possible. Nobunaga then sent a message to his brother about him being ill: "I have been taken with a sudden illness and my life is imperiled; come to me so that I can turn over to you headship of the family."[49] Nobuyuki left his Suemori Castle residence to see his brother. The result was an evil trick done by Nobunaga since he had Nobuyuki captured and was to take his own life in 1557.[50]

His treatment of his brother was harsh, brutal, and cunning! In order for Nobunaga to have complete control of the Oda family, he had to act quickly. There was no room for two people to run the clan. Only the fittest, strongest, and smartest survived in a time where the sword was the law of the land. Was Nobunaga's plan to kill his brother ruthless? Yes! In order for him to fortify his dream to unite the Oda clan and country, it was unavoidable.

Considerable that Nobunaga actually forgave Nobuyuki the first time he revolted against him.[51] The second time Nobuyuki took up arms Nobunaga took care of business. He had several more family members to deal with, although without the drama. His older brother, Nobuhiro, knowing he could receive the same fate as Nobuyuki, submitted to the fool. The last remaining Oda clan member, Nobukata attacked and killed in 1560 (1559?).[52] Another intriguing samurai was Shibata Katsuie. He was a vassal of Nobuyuki, but actually informed Nobunaga about his brother's plot.[53] From then on Shibata Katsuie was one of Nobunaga's most highly respected and loyal generals.

In 1557, Nobunaga had his first son, Nobutada. His mother, Kitsuno came from the Ikoma family and she was one of several Nobunaga's lovely concubines. She was Ikoma Ienaga's daughter and was a beautiful and sweet woman at the time. Kitsuno gave birth to Nobunaga's second son, Nobukatsu and his first daughter, Gotoku. He was born one year after Nobutada and Gotoku in 1559. As for Kitsuno, she tragically passed away in 1566 at Komaki Castle and buried at Kyūshōji. Nobunaga was in tears of heartbreak and deeply loved her.

In 1558, Nobunaga pitted against Oda Nobukata, the lord of Iwakura. The Battle of Ukino was located in Owari, present day Ichinomiya (Aichi Prefecture).[54] With the battle starting around noon, it seemed that Nobukata's men poorly positioned and disciplined.[55] Nobunaga sent some of his foot soldiers to test the strength of the enemy. He went for the kill after his soldiers returned to him.

The engagement was intense as various samurai, according to the *Shinchō-Kō ki*, fought with valor. A fight took place between two men, Hayashi Yashichirō and Hashimoto Ippa. According to the *Shinchō-Kō ki*, Hayashi was skilled with the bow and Hashimoto was skilled with the gun.[56]

The two men were rather familiar with each other. Hayashi was ready to fight and fired his arrows at his opponent. Hit was Hashimoto in the armpit, but was able to his fire twice at Hayashi.[57] One of Nobunaga's pages thought Hayashi was dead. The reason for the page, Sawaki Yoshiyuki, was to take Hayashi's head as a prize. Hayashi was not dead and cut Sawaki's hand. Fighting continued as Sawaki retaliated by taking Hayashi's head, bow, and sword.[58] The sword, according to the *Shinchō-Kō ki*, was famous.[59] The engagement ended up as a victory and the next day Nobunaga held a head viewing ceremony at Kiyosu Castle taking in 1,250 decapitated heads.[60]

In 1559, Nobunaga made his first trip to Kyoto. He was entertained by then, by shogun Ashikaga Yoshiteru. Nobunaga left Kiyosu in the middle of January and on 2 February 1559 he met the shogun. He also went to Nara and Sakai as a sightseeing trip as well. He would not return to the capital until 1568 with the fifteenth and last Ashikaga shogun Yoshiaki. After meeting with the shogun, Nobunaga returned home. The Kyoto visit by Nobunaga might have pulled the trigger for Yoshimoto to prepare his crusade for the capital.

Noted down in the *Shinchō-Kō ki* was that the Saitō clan headed by Yoshitatsu hired men from Mikawa to kill Nobunaga.[61] The plot to assassinate Nobunaga was obvious. (1) Nobunaga's alliance with the Saitō was broken in 1556 when Dōsan was killed, (2) hiring men from Mikawa (presumably from the Imagawa), an enemy domain was a logical choice for Yoshitatsu, and (3) if the plot were successful, Nobunaga's Owari domain would be very weak. However, the plot was not successful and Nobunaga would have the last laugh.

In early spring of 1559, Nobunaga attacked Iwakura Castle. Iwakura was the last stand for the original Oda family (Oda Iwakura branch) in Owari. For three months, he assaulted the castle with everything he possessed. Fire arrows and matchlock rifles played a pivotal role. He set the town ablaze as people fled the castle area. Oda Nobukata finally gave up when he knew it was a lost cause and surrendered. Nobunaga gave the order to demolish Iwakura Castle before returning to Kiyosu.

Nobunaga's conquest was significant considering it accomplished the job of uniting Owari in his name. Oda Nobuhide never finished the task before he passed away and the result was a civil war in Owari. He completed the mission that paved the way for future glory and was new ruler of Owari.

2

Before Okehazama
Oda and Imagawa Battles

THE Imagawa and the Oda had bad blood between them. Even though Nobunaga would have the last laugh in 1560, his father Nobuhide fought the Imagawa with mixed results. In 1542, Nobuhide and the Imagawa clan mixed it up at Azuki-kura, near Okazaki.[62] Nobuhide triumphed, but it will be only a few years later when the two will square off again at the same place (1548). One year earlier (1547), Nobunaga had his first baptism of war against the Imagawa. His father had troubling times trying fending off the Imagawa from the rear and the Saitō from the front.

Azuki-kura in 1542 was no walk in the park. According to the *Shinchō-Kō ki*, the battle was violent with high casualties.[63] The Imagawa was advancing to Shodawara while Nobuhide was protecting Anjō Castle. Both armies met at Azuki-kura and fought. The result was a narrow victory, according to the *Oda Nobunaga Sōgō Jiten*.[64] *The Mikawa Monogatari* had a different view on the battle and considering the way it looked as if the Imagawa won the conflict.[65] Victory or not, the meaningful part was both families were fighting against one another. Both sides were taking castles and forts here and there, but they could not topple one another until 1560.

The second battle and the year after had much more drama since it would involve young Ieyasu and Yoshimoto's famed military man Taigen Sūfu (Kyūeishōgiku). Sūfu played a key role because the victory would go to the Imagawa. As for young Ieyasu, it meant he would serve the Imagawa until Yoshimoto's death. The *Shinchō-Kō ki* had nothing about the second battle and Gyūichi failed to write anything about it. Was it important to Gyūichi? Apparently, it was not significant to him.

Oda Nobuhide lost Anjō Castle in 1549 and captured was his son Nobuhiro.[66] The two clans agreed to exchange hostages with the help of Sūfu and Ieyasu was included in the swap. Ieyasu spent two years at Atsuta and he was a hostage once again, but for the Imagawa. Months earlier before the siege, Ieyasu's father, Hirotada, suddenly passed away. He ended up assassinated by one of his retainers. After Hirotada's death, the Matsudaira family was in shambles until Ieyasu was able to clean it up after the Battle of Okehazama. For Nobuhide, it was an embarrassment considering he assaulted Anjō nine years earlier (1540), which the Matsudaira controlled at the time.

Muraki and Terabe

Nobunaga had a major victory over the Imagawa six years earlier. Explained since his conquest in 1554, the Battle of Muraki was due to matchlock rifles. His triumph was more impressive since the European rifle first arrived in Japan in 1543 and he swiftly made use of them.

As for the year of the battle itself, there was a slight difference. Owada's *Okehazama no Tatakai* the battle listed as 1553. The *Shinchō-Kō ki* had the year listed in 1554. Owada was not wrong. His work included other sources that had the year 1554. As for this book, the year stands at 1554.

During the New Year in 1554, Imagawa Yoshimoto dispatched his army and took over Shigihara Castle in Okazaki.[67] After taking the castle, the army planned to assault Nobunaga's castle of Ogawa, held by Mizuno Kingo Tadamasa. The Imagawa army started to build fortifications at Muraki, and had a temple ally, Teramoto. Nobunaga expeditiously heard the major news and prepared for war. Nobunaga knew if he pushed on to Ogawa from Nagoya by land, the Imagawa would cut off his army, so instead he departed from Nagoya by boat. Afterwards he requested much needed help from his father-in-law, Saitō Dōsan.

On 18 January 1554, Ando Iga no Kami (Morinari) with a thousand men including, Tamiya, Kabutoyama, Anzai, Kumazawa, Monodari Shingo guarded Nagoya Castle and provided information daily to Dōsan.[68] On the twentieth, Nobunaga and the Oda army greeted Ando Morinari.

The next day Nobunaga made war plans, although some of his soldiers questioned his motives. Hayashi Shingorō, his brother Mimasaka no Kami, and Maeda Yujurō of Arako protested; however, Nobunaga said, "Go!"[69] Nobunaga stayed at Atsuta on the twenty-first and he rode his horse,"Monokawa" into town. The next day the Oda army crossed the Chita Hantō from Atsuta by boat and arrived at the Ogawa stronghold. The wind was potent and so strong, noted in the *Shinchō-Kō ki*, the winds were identical with the Genpei Wars (*Genpei Monogatari*).[70] Intriguing enough, it only took an hour to cross. Why travel by boat? As mentioned earlier, Nobunaga had to move by boat so the Imagawa could not cut off his army, which would have been a catastrophe.

Combat began in the early morning, 24 January, and Nobunaga already had issues. The north end of the castle heavily supported with troops east was the entrance, and west of the castle the exit. The south had a mighty deep moat and would be extremely difficult to cross.[71] Nobunaga had his army attack the castle's formidable south side, but his legions easily slaughtered. While Nobunaga pushed back, he then came up with an idea to use his matchlock guns. His use of matchlock rifles was highly effective at Muraki. He used the rotating volley method so proficiently the Imagawa army suffered heavy casualties. His dynamic use of this new weapon would separate him from the rest of the warlords in Japan. This made him special and unique during the Sengoku Era.

Fighting continued into the early evening. After a short break, Nobunaga continued to press his men to fight. The Imagawa army ran out of gas and the triumphant Nobunaga rejoices. His superior use of firearms and strong will at the Battle of Muraki were the key factors. Nobunaga wanted the victory more than the Imagawa. At the same time, he paid a heavy price for the victory. Nobunaga was in tears when many of his young pages and soldiers bravely died for him.[72] Victory was never cheap in Sengoku Japan. The price always paid in blood.

Set on fire was Teramoto on 25 January, and Nobunaga returned to Nagoya the next day to meet and praise Ando Morinari.

One person who had mixed feelings on Nobunaga's triumph was Dōsan. He was delighted to see his son-in-law safe, yet at the same time, a little concerned. He was worried right from the start since he knew Nobunaga was young and daring.

Nobunaga triumphed; his army would get stronger, and would get more ambitious. Nobunaga embarrassed his father-in-law less than a year ago. The meeting still must have been fresh in his head and bold enough to try to take over Mino. Ando Morinari returned to Mino on 27 January while Nobunaga returned to Owari.[73]

For the Imagawa, it would be a prelude to what to come next from Nobunaga. Yoshimoto never knew Nobunaga's talents as a war strategist. Instead, he thought Nobunaga was just another country boy idiot. His attitude towards Nobunaga was pure stupidity, and unlike Dōsan, who knew his rare talents and was not afraid to use it. Yoshimoto did not regret his mistake and would later become the great fool.

One-engagement historians often overlook and do not pay much attention to is Kanie Castle. In 1555, Yoshimoto's army (consisted of Mikawa soldiers) assaulted Kanie, which was in Nobunaga's province of Owari. The battle occurred before Nobunaga ruled Owari for good in 1559. Led by Matsudaira Chikanori, the army crossed Ise Bay on and attacked Kanie, which the Sakuma family occupied. The assault on Kanie was a retaliation of the Muraki loss one year earlier.

A troubling year was 1558 for the two families, but Yoshimoto had a legitimate gripe. One of Yoshimoto's soldiers deserted him and joined the Oda. Suzuki Shigeteru was the man who forced Yoshimoto to pull the trigger against Nobunaga in

1558. He would not send out his own army to try to settle the matter with Nobunaga, but would send young Ieyasu instead. Yoshimoto told Motoyasu:

Western Mikawa has always been your territory and now Suzuki Shigeteru, lord of the castle of Terabe, has deserted us and gone over to Oda Nobunaga with it. How awful![74]

Ieyasu organized his army and attacked Terabe. Terabe was a tough nut to crack. They were able to burn and destroyed the outer linings, but the main castle proved too difficult.[75] The outer linings of Terabe had to be the san no maru (the third outer ring of the castle) since noted in the *Mikawa Monogatari*.[76] Along with the san no maru burned, many soldiers received casualties. Ieyasu then attacked the rear with success, but Nobunaga heard about the plans, and he sent a force to repel it.[77] Sadler portrayed the siege as a victory for Ieyasu. Was it a victory? Yes, however Ieyasu was not able to control the castle himself.

If Sadler's view taken as a victory for Motoyasu (Ieyasu); thus, it was a victory since the Imagawa showed the fool they would not sit back and wait. He was upset Terabe in his own hands; however, lost the castle as one of his own switched sides.

Nobunaga still had control of Terabe and that was the most important result of the battle. Yoshimoto did congratulate Ieyasu on his work and presented him with a sword and 300 kwan of land.[78] The land that granted was Ieyasu's own. Yoshimoto would not dare to give up any land of his ownership. His objective was to destabilize the Matsudaira and Ieyasu's power. Then he would take over Mikawa once weakened. Ieyasu's men pleaded with Yoshimoto that their lord return to them.[79] The request was denied by and a clever move on his part. Ieyasu was rapidly establishing himself as a capable leader and soldier. More important, Yoshimoto was shrewd enough to recognize it.

Another engagement took place the same year (7 March 1558) and it was against the same family, the Matsudaira. The Imagawa army held Shinano Castle in present day Aichi Prefecture. Matsudaira Ietsugu was the commander of the castle. Nobunaga was able to lay siege to the castle and scores slaughtered. Owada Tetsuo used the *Matsudaira-ki* for his interpretation of the battle.[80] What was significant about the battle? Nobunaga had a castle occupied by the Imagawa in his domain near the Mikawa border. The situation would become uneasy before the eruption. Both sides exchanged skirmishes, which would gradually lead to Yoshimoto's plan to crush Nobunaga and occupy Kyoto.

Last was a small clash two weeks before the Battle of Okehazama. Nobunaga and the Imagawa had a small skirmish at The Battle of Mikawa Kira, which took place on 5 May 1560. It was the same area where Nobunaga fought his first engagement in 1547. Okada Masahito's *Oda Nobunaga Sōgō Jiten* noted the action as a "preliminary skirmish to Okehazama."[81] Okada used the *Okazaki Kōki* as his source on the battle and not noted in the *Shinchō-Kō ki*.[82] If the battle did take place, Nobunaga had to know there was a high possibility the Imagawa was going to invade Owari sooner not later.

Nobunaga's Army Before Okehazama

Magistrate Group	Red Cowl Group
Matsui Yūkan	Maeda Toshiie
Murai Sadakatsu	Azai Shinpachi
Shimada Hidemitsu	Mōri Nagahide
Ikeyama Nobukatsu	Iwamuro Nagatono
Sofue Hideshige	Iio Hisakyo
Myōin Ryōsei	Hasegawa Hashisuke
	Yamaguchi Hida no Kami
	Itō Seizo
	Sawaki Yoshiyuki
	Kinoshita Yoshitoshi

Black Cowl Group	Adult Group
Sasa Narimasa	Asano Nagakatsu
Kawajiri Hidetaka	Ōta Gyūichi
Hirai Kyūemon	Hotta Kazutsugu
Mōri Yoshikatsu	Itō Seizo
Nakagawa Shigemasa	
Matsuoka Kurōjirō	
Mizuno Tatewaki	
Ikoma Katsusuke	

Generals Group	Chief Retainer Group
Shibata Katsuie	Hayashi Hidesada
Oda Nobufusa	Oda Hidetoshi
Oda Nobukiyo	**Pages**
Sakuma Nobumori	Iwamuro Nagato no Kami
Sakuma Morishige	Hasegawa Hashisuke
Oda Hiroyoshi	Yamaguchi Hida no Kami
Wada Shinsuke	Sawaki Yoshiyuki
Nakajima Bungo no Kami	Gatō Yasaburō

Nobunaga's army expanded after Okehazama. Jeroen Lamers pointed out that according to the *Shinchō-Kō ki* Nobunaga had less than a thousand troops and defeated Shibata Katsuie, who led a bigger army in 1556.[83] The name of the battle was the Battle of Inō in Owari. According to Lamers, after Nobunaga killed his brother, the men joined his legion. Thus, creating the small army that was enough to control his domain, but nothing compared to the mighty Imagawa. Bandits on the loose who decided to join the Oda army were favorable for Nobunaga. Men such as Maeda Toshiie, Sakuma Nobumori (later banished for too many mishaps), Ikeda Tsuneoki, and Shibata Katsuie were important people in Nobunaga's army. These men along with Mōri Shinsuke and several others participated with Nobunaga at the Battle of Okehazama, and were central to his victory.

1558 was the year young Hideyoshi defected the Imagawa and joined the Oda, according to Mary Elizabeth Berry.[84] She also said joining the Imagawa was "curious" because his father had served under the Oda.[85] Nobunaga used the boys from Owari throughout his career who were familiar with him and his tactics. More significantly, the boys from Owari would form the backbone of Nobunaga's army. Almost all of them promoted on military merit and not on family lineage.

3
Yoshimoto before Okehazama

BEFORE Okehazama, Yoshimoto made alliances with the Hōjō in Odawara (east) and Takeda in Kai (north) in order to strengthen his control of Suruga and Mikawa.[86] According to Berry, Yoshimoto's daughter married Takeda Shingen's son, Shingen's daughter married Hōjō's son, and Hōjō's daughter married Yoshimoto's son (Ujizane).[87] The daughter who wed Ujizane was Hayakawa-dono. Shingen was suspicious because Yoshimoto did provide refuge for Takeda Nobutora (Shingen's father) whom he ousted in 1541. All three families have fought against or for each other; however, a triple peace pact created planned after the Hōjō made a run at Suruga while Imagawa was invading Mikawa. The Takeda jumped in to help the Imagawa and repelled the Hōjō. [88]

Yoshimoto was shrewd enough to mediate between the Hōjō, Takeda, and diplomacy was a strong point of his. The mediation allowed him the opportunity to march to the capital, which was significant. Nevertheless, was he capable enough to fight his way to Kyoto? That was the main question and Yoshimoto ended up failing the test at Okehazama. He was no natural soldier and it was one his many shortcomings. However, he was much better than his lame son Ujizane.

Continue with the Takeda considering it had some issues. Yoshimoto's wife Jōkeiin, married in 1537, but she passed away in 1550 at the age of thirty-two. Yoshimoto's wife was Takeda Shingen's sister and her father was Takeda Nobutora.[89] The alliance was in peril, but two years later Yoshimoto's daughter married Takeda Shingen's oldest son Yoshinobu. As for the Hōjō and the Takeda, their marriages took place in 1554 and the triple pact stated earlier between the three clans was done same year at Zentokuji by Taigen Sūfu.

If the Hōjō and the Takeda wanted their wishes granted they too would like to occupy Kyoto, they had problems doing it. First, the Hōjō and the Takeda were too far from the capital, a major handicap. The Takeda, on the other hand, had other issues to deal with. Shingen was endlessly at war with Uesugi Kenshin of Echigo and it would be only one year later the two would meet up at Kawanakajima (area around Nagano) in 1561 for the fourth time.

Shingen had intentions to put his banner in Kyoto, yet Nobunaga, Ieyasu, and Kenshin were the main threat to him. The movie *Kagemusha* displayed Shingen's lost opportunity for Kyoto when he had the chance. If the Hōjō, Uesugi, and the Takeda were not preoccupied with other affairs, not geographically disadvantaged, yet they might have changed Yoshimoto's blueprint of occupying the capital.

Yoshimoto was a highly enlightened man who was known for his scented hair and blacked teeth in a style that as a courtier.[90]

Sadler illustrated Yoshimoto's physique as "...long-bodied short-legged little man, with long hair..."[91] His mansion was supposed be a replica of the capital Kyoto.[92] He was so fond of the capital that the surrounding areas and buildings such as beauty shops named after famous places in Kyoto.[93] As a case in point, in Owada Tetsuo's book, *Imagawa Yoshimoto*, designated Sunpu as the "East Capital."[94] It additionally had a replica of Kyoto's Kiyomizu Temple as well.

In all honesty, the Imagawa clan and others benefited from the Ōnin War from the previous century.[95] Part of the cultural elite fled Kyoto and expanded their work to other provinces in Japan.[96] This exodus of Kyoto's cultural elite provided the seeds that would later developed into the Japan we know today. For example, the Japanese tea ceremony and the Nō play spread throughout the nation.

As for the Imagawa family itself, their power came from the Ashikaga shogunate.[97] The Imagawa family was the governor (shugo) of Suruga from 1337 until the fall of the clan in the 1560s. Imagawa might was the endless control in their own province away from the capital which created a stable administration.[98] The result was their house laws that created steadiness in the Imagawa governed provinces.

Yoshimoto was ninth member of the Imagawa headship. Others before him were in power during the late fifteenth and early sixteenth century. They included the fourth, Norimasa; fifth, Noritada; sixth, Yoshitada; seventh, Ujichika (1473-1526); and eighth, Ujiteru (1513-1536).[99]

Yoshimoto's love for Kyoto had to come from his early days as a young boy. Known as Hōgikumaru, his childhood name, Yoshimoto was born in 1519.[100] In the 1530s, he spent time at Kyoto's Kenninji and Myōshinji, and studied Zen there. During that time, Sengakushōhō was his name.[101] There he had to be accustomed to the lavish Kyoto lifestyle.

By 1536, Yoshimoto took over the Imagawa clan due to a dispute with his half brother Genkōetan. Clan chaos erupted when Ujiteru unexpectedly passed away at the tender age of twenty-four in 1536. Genkōetan was third in line and Yoshimoto was the fifth son of Ujichika. In fact, Genkōetan's mother was Ujichika's concubine. She was Kushima Saemon's daughter. The Kushima family was solid during the time. It was a prime example of daily life in Sengoku Japan. The clan was fighting for power and canceling each other out. Creating a vacuum where Yoshimoto took over the clan. He won the Battle of Hanakura Castle (Fujieda City), which forced Genkōetan to flee and take his own life at Fumonji.

This was a historic victory for Yoshimoto. He was able to gain total control of the Imagawa house. The man who was supposed to live the religious life was now a Sengoku warlord. More significant, his name changed to Yoshimoto in 1536. "Yoshi" came from the twelfth Ashikaga shogun Yoshiharu.[102] Yoshimoto's titles included, the Fox of Suruga (nickname), Imagawa Chibudaifu Yoshimoto, Kazusa no Suke, and Mikawa no Kami.

Yoshimoto's mother was no slouch either. She was the daughter of a Court noble, and according to Sadler, and her father's name was Dainagon Naka-no-mikado Nobutane.[103]

Sadler made the point in his book, *The Maker of Modern Japan*, it was Yoshimoto's wife, but the fact it was his mother, Jukeini, who was the daughter of the Court noble.[104] She married Yoshimoto's father Ujichika, in the early 1500s. Jukeini was further known as Ōkata-dono in her early life and she passed away in 1568.

A mother born, raised in Kyoto, and from the aristocracy made the perfect match for Yoshimoto since he loved to live like a couturier this included noble blood from his mother. Ujichika's older sister was married to Ōgimachi Sanjō Sanemochi.[105] Marriage to the upper class made the Imagawa family secure. To live such a lavish lifestyle must have been costly and no doubt Yoshimoto left the to the Sunpu peasants.[106]

Yoshimoto was renowned for his land surveys. He did it because he wanted to know more about his lands in Suruga. It showed his administration skills were on par at the time. The land surveys were to show which areas had the highest rice production and where taxes gathered. Taxes collected used for his rich lifestyle. As for Kyoto campaign, he had the necessary resources for such an operation.

He continued to expand the laws that his father wrote, *Kana Mokuroku Tsuika*, that would establish local rule. The laws were so important that it would help create a strong and independent rule of government.[107] Ujichika must have written and issued around thirty-three articles in 1526, and Yoshimoto added twenty-one in 1553.[108] More significantly, not only the Imagawa made laws, but other clans did too.[109]

The difference between Nobunaga and Yoshimoto's childhood was so concrete; it played a role at Okehazama.

Nobunaga did not live the pampered life compared to Yoshimoto. He loved to play around with his friends and create mischief. Yoshimoto, on the other hand, was accustomed to the opulent Kyoto lifestyle. His character and lifestyle was that of a Kyoto aristocrat. He had a much more disciplined childhood than Nobunaga. On the contrary, Nobunaga treated society based on character and did not care where the masses came from. One more consequential character difference between the two: Nobunaga was a true warrior, a country boy; however, Yoshimoto was the complete opposite, an elitist.

As stated earlier, he was no natural soldier compared to Nobunaga and had to rely on others such as Sūfu and Ieyasu. His dream was vanished and made matters much worse for the Imagawa since there was a quick decaying in power after Yoshimoto's death.

To sum it up, Yoshimoto was able to get his rivals to compromise a peace pact. He had to be a decent politician to get the job done. His listening and speaking skills were excellent enough to persuade the Hōjō and Takeda to follow through. The work must have been difficult and the alliance prevented further bloodshed. When the big test came, he failed since his military arts were weak.

Taigen Sūfu

Taigen Sūfu (Sessai) was a brilliant Zen monk-war tactician. He lived and studied in Kyoto for his training. First at Kenninji (Kyoto's first Zen temple, founded in 1202 by Eisai of the Rinzai school) and later became the abbot at Myōshinji. He then returned to Suruga to work for the Imagawa. There he acted as the abbot of the Rinzaiji Temple at Sunpu, according to Sadler.[110]

Sūfu's administration skills were superb in his day. He often played a mediator for Yoshimoto in diplomatic situations for the Imagawa clan.[111] For example, he helped solidify the triple peace pact in 1554 with the Hōjō and Takeda for Yoshimoto before his death one year later (known as the Kōsōsun Dōmei).[112] Zentokuji (located in Fuji City) was the place where all three families met and solidified the pact. Yoshimoto spent some of his early days as a young boy at Zentokuji. As for the temple itself, its historical roots date back to the Kamakura Era. It was Suruga's Rinzai sect branch temple. It was the perfect place for the meeting since it was close to Sunpu and the temple is now a simple park landmark.

The triple pact Sūfu completed allowed Yoshimoto to plan the march to Kyoto. Without the triple pact, Yoshimoto's march to the capital would have only been a dream. Sūfu did his part. His pupil now had the hard part: fighting his way to Kyoto. He additionally served as Yoshimoto's military adviser. Sūfu's military skills were superb and his participation in battles such as Azuki-kura 1548 and Anjō in 1549 were pivotal to the Imagawa.

Sūfu was not able to see Yoshimoto's failed Kyoto campaign since passed away at the age sixty at Chōkeiji Temple in 1555 (in modern day Fujieda City). Replacing him would be a daunting task and reality proved it. Yoshimoto never replaced him and he had to be terrified. Yoshimoto had to do the job alone and was not able to do it. In conclusion, it was a blessing Sūfu did not see the Okehazama debacle.

4
Okehazama: The Early Stages

THE Battle of Okehazama in 1560 is one of great significance in Japanese military history since it involved two warlords. The two could have not been more different. Nobunaga was a true warrior and Yoshimoto, the man who had to decide between aristocrat and warrior. It would be Nobunaga's finest hour since his forces were completely outnumbered almost twelve or thirteen to one in terms of military might. In historic terms: Nobunaga's superior use of intelligence would change Sengoku warfare forever. The real battle took place in a gorge of Dengaku-hazama, yet named the Battle of Okehazama since it was the nearest town by the battlefield.

After unifying Owari, Nobunaga tried to invade the province of Mino. Yoshimoto who had the same desire to rule the nation of Japan restrained Nobunaga's attempt.[113] Yoshimoto held the domain from the rear and Nobunaga had to think twice if he wanted to head up north to capture Mino.

How many men marched with Yoshimoto on his campaign to Kyoto? The *Shinchō-Kō ki* noted down the Imagawa army had around 45,000 troops.[114] The numbers are staggering and overpowering. If one wanted to argue Yoshimoto did bring around 45,000 troops, one must recognize in 1568, when Nobunaga went to claim his authority in Kyoto, he brought around 60,000 troops, according to Lamers's *Japonius Tyrannus*.[115]   Other chronicles such as the *Hōjō go dai ki*, interpreted the Imagawa army consisted of 25,000 men.[116]   A more probable amount of men since the document is close to the actual number.

Whatever the number of soldiers noted down, it appeared and was dead on accurate Nobunaga was outnumbered. The book, *Oda Nobunaga no Subete* explained the Imagawa army had around two or three thousand samurai with the remaining army consisted of lower class soldiers.[117] The ashigaru or foot soldiers would do the dirty work and was the backbone of the mighty Imagawa army.

The question remains as to what was Yoshimoto's main objective - Kyoto, or overtaking Nobunaga and Owari. Historians recently have made the claim Yoshimoto's goal was Owari. Movies, novels, and war chronicles have pointed out that Yoshimoto's intention was Kyoto.   Both arguments are valid. Mitsuo Kure's *Samurai: An Illustrated History*, made the point Yoshimoto's goal was only to make his mark in Owari and take out Nobunaga.[118] Disagree with Kure's theory whereas with over 25,000 soldiers proceeding along with Yoshimoto himself made the point Kyoto was his goal. Twenty-five thousand soldiers were more than adequate for the Kyoto campaign. If he only wanted to take over Owari, he could have sent less since Nobunaga was still not strong enough to take on the massive Imagawa army.

Here is a solution to create Kure's theory. If Yoshimoto occupied Owari long enough to provide the necessary logistics; then, it could be used as a future springboard to Kyoto. What Kure failed to mention was Yoshimoto's fanatical obsession with the ancient city.

Another case for Nobunaga and Owari was Owada Tetsuo's *Imagawa Yoshimoto*. He mentioned the Sengoku daimyo's main objective was to expand territory within their own and others (agree), and (Yoshimoto) retaking Nagoya Castle.[119] Explained will be Nagoya Castle. It appeared that the Imagawa held the citadel until Oda Nobuhide took it over in the 1530s. Yoshimoto's father, Ujichika, built the castle for his younger son Ujitoyo. Furthermore, Okada Masahito's *Oda Nobunaga Sōgō Jiten* noted Nobuhide assaulted the Imagawa stronghold in 1538.[120] There was a possibility that the castle assaulted in 1532.

Owada listed four key points in his book, *Imagawa Yoshimoto no Subete*. He noted down Kyoto, secure Mikawa, secure Narumi-Ōdaka line, and capture Owari.[121] All are four points reasonable and well thought-out. He made the case; however, still think Kyoto was Yoshimoto's main ambition. It was every Sengoku warlord's dream to occupy the capital. For Yoshimoto, it was his destiny.

It was only a year earlier Uesugi Kenshin with five thousand troops arrived in Kyoto in 1559 to visit the shogun Ashikaga Yoshiteru, and it was his second time (first in 1553). The same year Nobunaga visited Yoshiteru in Kyoto (1559) with less than a hundred men, but under different circumstances. One theory could be Yoshimoto alarmed by Kenshin's second arrival in Kyoto and Nobunaga's visit as well.[122] He had to do something himself to stake a claim in the capital quickly.

Yoshimoto held huge a geographical advantage over his rivals. Takeda Shingen locked in the mountains of Kai, the Hōjō were too far east, and Uesugi Kenshin was in constant battle with Shingen and with the warrior monks. The Saitō were vying with the Oda and Yoshimoto's advance was quick enough to alarm the surrounding warlords about his intentions. After all, he had little respect for Nobunaga anyway.

Yoshimoto's Kyoto Campaign Begins

Preparations for the Kyoto crusade began in late April or early May and Yoshimoto departed his Sunpu headquarters (modern day Shizuoka City) on 12 May 1560. Debated is the day he departed. For example, Owada Tetsuo stated that the *Isokuhōshi Monogatari* and the *Chōyakyūbunhōkō* Yoshimoto departed on the tenth.[123] Accepted is the day that Yoshimoto left for Kyoto on the twelfth with the main army. Ii Naomori, the lord of Ii no ya Castle, (Shizuoka Prefecture) along with young Ieyasu departed on the tenth with Yoshimoto's troops and the allied army heading west.

Yoshimoto's army stayed in Fujieda and on the thirteenth advanced to Kakegawa Castle. The Asahina family governed the castle. On 14 May, he departed early in the morning from Kakekawa Castle, crossed the Tenryū River, and arrived at Hikuma Castle (Hamamatsu City), occupied by the Inō family.

Hikuma Castle clarified in context of its name. Almost ten years later Ieyasu would change the castle to Hamamatsu. He attacked Hikuma in 1568, and by 1570, the name was changed. The name Hikuma did have a negative touch to it. Hikuma means, "pulling the reigns" (as in retreat) and Ieyasu was right to change the name to its present form to Hamamatsu, Hikuma Castle: same location-different name.

On the night of the fifteenth, Yoshimoto arrived at Yoshida Castle governed by the Itō family (Toyohashi City, Aichi Prefecture). The sixteenth, Yoshimoto and his army arrived at night at Okazaki Castle, which was Ieyasu's headquarters. This was significant considering he had to lodge his lord who did not have any love loss towards the Matsudaira clan. Okazaki would help delay Ieyasu's move back home when Yoshimoto perished at Okehazama. Imagawa soldiers who were stationed there might have been reinforcements for Yoshimoto in case of an emergency.

Yoshimoto extended his war campaign to Chiryū and crossed the Sakai River on 17 May. His final stop before heading off to Ōdaka was Kutsukake Castle, which was possible that he arrived in the afternoon, and covered around 6.2 miles or ten kilos.[124] It is possible Yoshimoto arrived in the afternoon if he left Chiryū early in the morning. Owada Tetsuo mentioned two documents, *Chōyakūbunhōkō* and *Okehazama Kassenki*, did not have any mention at all about the time arrival.[125] Why it might be necessary, the time noted down. If he did arrive at Kutsukake Castle in the afternoon Yoshimoto had the space to rest his troops and prepare for work the next day.

Kondō Kageharu commanded Kutsukake Castle. Kondō Munemitsu first governed the castle in 1325. Kageharu served under Matsudaira Hirotada in his early years and he was the ninth lord of the citadel. After Okehazama, killed was Kageharu when Nobunaga assaulted the castle. During those six days, Yoshimoto went through three provinces: Tōtōmi, Mikawa, and Owari.[126] He had little or no resistance heading west until he arrives at Nobunaga's Owari domain.

The lack resistance was significant because the pace of the campaign was rapid. Yoshimoto had to be pleased whereas if the campaign continued at the same pace, he would arrive in Kyoto in early June. On the other hand, his troops were not tested and it would come back to haunt the army at the Battle of Okehazama. Nobunaga did have a chain of forts in Owari besides Kiyosu Castle. Several forts would play a critical role during the battle. The five forts are Tange, Zenshōji, Nakajima, Marune, and Washizu. Even if all the forts combined into one army, it was still less than Yoshimoto's main army. Owada Tetsuo was brilliant enough to include the main generals who occupied the forts and the number soldiers stationed there.

Tange, Mizuno Tatewaki, Yamaguchi Ebi no Jō, Maki Yōjūrō, Maki Sōjūrō, Ban Jū zaemon and Tsugegen Ban no Kami; Zenshōji, Sakuma Nobumori and Sakuma Chikamori; Nakajima, Kajikawa Takahide; Marune, Sakuma Morishige (Daigaku); Washizu, Oda Nobushige, Inō Sadamune, and Inō Oki no Kami.[127] The number of soldiers stationed at each fort: Tange, 340; Zenshōji, 450; Nakajima, 250; Marune, 150; and Washizu, 520. [128]

The numbers varied, but Owada Tetsuo's *Okehazama no Tatakai* did provide the data. Owada tried to tell the reader

Nobunaga was considerably in trouble when Marune and Washizu fell into Imagawa hands.

Nobunaga was keen enough to know the forts had a purpose. For example, Tange, Zenshōji, and Nakajima built to balance out Narumi. Tange was north of Narumi, Zenshōji east, and Nakajima south. Marune and Washizu built to counter against Ōdaka. Washizu was to counter Ōdaka and Narumi, and Marune was to counter Ōdaka and Kutsukake. The castles were not on the coastline, which forced Yoshimoto to go inland and attack the forts before taking Kiyosu. Time was critical. The forts gave him enough time to assemble a small army for an ambush opportunity.

The Imagawa and allied army continued to push through Mikawa and the Owari frontier where his two dwellings of Narumi on the Tōkaidō road and Ōdaka south of it stood the five forts Nobunaga erected. Diminished the five forts had to be before any further acceleration. Marune and Washizu were close to Ōdaka and Yoshimoto had no other choice but to smoke them out.

Ieyasu and Ōdaka

Yoshimoto instructed Ieyasu, who was in the service of Imagawa at the time, to deliver provisions to Ōdaka by baggage train (use of animals).[129] The job was not attractive or glamorous. However, it was a considerable task and he did it without any complaints. Ieyasu replied, "That's the sort of duty I like," "And I shall be equally ready to undertake at any time these difficult jobs that other leaders don't care for."[130] In short, Ieyasu was happy to do it. Chores similar to the one mentioned above made him stand out from other leaders who were too timid. Sugawara Makoto's article "Heroes of the Unification of the Country" in *The East*, noted that Ieyasu delivered 450 bags of rice.[131]

Ōdaka was an Imagawa castle that was in desperate need of supplies such as rice and other foodstuffs. When Ieyasu launched his attack, most of the Oda forces withdrew a decent amount of men from Ōdaka.[132] The castle was relieved when Ieyasu arrived and waited for Yoshimoto who expected to show up the next day late in the afternoon. Before Ieyasu arrived and carried out his orders, he was able to meet his mother and her siblings.[133] The meeting was emotional since he was not able see his mother in sixteen years.

Ieyasu separated from his mother, Ōdai, when he was about a year old. According to Lamers, Ōdai came from the Mizuno family who had strong ties with the Oda.[134] Ieyasu's father, Hirotada, had to decide if he still wanted a strong relationship with the Imagawa after a Mizuno command change, which became more pro Oda.[135] Hirotada decided to stay with the Imagawa. Ōdai had to return to the Mizuno and the Matsudaira continued their relationship with the Imagawa.

If anything that stood out and was a revelation, it was Ieyasu's body armor. His armor was gold lacquered and according to Stephen Turnbull, armor was usually black or brown, but Ieyasu's was gold.[136] His armor was not flashy, yet simple.

There was some confusion about Ieyasu's arrival at Ōdaka Castle. For example, according to the *Mikawa Monogatari*, Ieyasu's supply train arrived two years earlier.[137] The *Shinchō-Kō ki* stated that he arrived at night before the battle.[138] Owada Tetsuo also stated the two sources but with the day before Okehazama (18 May) as the correct date.[139] The correct date was 18 May, because Ōdaka needed supplies and Ieyasu was ready to assault the Oda forts for Yoshimoto's crusade to Kyoto via Kiyosu.

There is speculation Hattori Hanzō, Japan's most famous ninja, helped Ieyasu deliver the supplies at night. According to the *Sengoku Bushō Retsuden*, Hanzō was a key man in taking charge of the task.[140] If Hanzō did participated in the event; then, he was with Ieyasu from the start. Hanzō achieved many feats for Ieyasu during his sparkling career.

Udono Nagateru did have a relationship with Yoshimoto. Nagateru's father, Nagamochi died in 1556 and his wife related to Yoshimoto and his son Ujizane.[141]   When Ieyasu arrived at Ōdaka, Nagateru replaced not because of bad blood, but for tactical reasons. A logical and possible tactic might have been the Udono army placed at Fort Marune after the siege since Ieyasu held Ōdaka Castle. The castle's defensive surroundings were by two moats. After Okehazama, abandoned was the citadel due to the lost strategic value.

Ieyasu made a night incursion on the two forts Marune and Washizu. At around three in the morning, the attack on Marune began.[142]   He had around 1000 soldiers to attack, but another account listed the army around 2,500.[143] The bloody hard fought battle; yet Ieyasu carried the provisions about a mile from Ōdaka.

Ieyasu stormed and scorched Fort Marnue with fierce fighting. Arriving at Fort Marune was smooth since it was near the Ōdaka Highway. According to Stephen Turnbull's *Battles of the Samurai*, Ieyasu constructed a battery position of guns and bows ready for the Oda attack.[144] As intense it was, it was an Ieyasu victory. A Mikawa sharpshooter allegedly killed the commander of Fort Marune, Sakuma Daigaku.[145]

One young soon to be famous samurai made his debut at the tender age of thirteen. Honda Tadakatsu received his first taste of war at the siege of Marune. Two other samurai, Ishikawa Ienari and Sakai Tadatsugu, led the siege of Marune.[146] Many of Ieyasu's men who survived the Okehazama blunder would serve under him in his early days as the defender of Mikawa.

Fort Washizu destroyed by the Imagawa and allied army led by Asahina Yasutomo and Ii Naomori, who led around 2,000 men, and looked as though the path to Nobunaga's domain was open.[147] There was speculation that Yasutomo and Naomori led around 6,000 troops. Owada's reference to the theory was the *Sakai Hon Mikawa-ki*, but he even stated the number was too high and the 2,000 soldiers were more accurate.[148] Killed in action was Inō Sadamune along with Oda Genba at Fort Washizu. After the siege of Fort Washizu, the Asahina army held the fort until further notice. Everything was going Yoshimoto's way with no sign of luck running out.

5

Nobunaga Prepares for War

NEWS reached Kiyosu as if Paul Revere was in Japan telling Nobunaga that the Imagawa are coming, and he was not worried at all. He had a trick up his sleeve and knew a way out of the sticky situation. The evening of 18 May, Nobunaga at Kiyosu Castle, was well aware the Imagawa allied army was destroying his forts. He informed the council of his master plan for war. His retainers had an indication the end was near for the clan; however, Nobunaga declared by allegedly saying, "fruitless to remain in the castle. We will take the field before daybreak. This is a kill-or-be-killed situation."[149] Kaku Kōzō's book, *Nobunaga no Nazo*, illustrated the same thing what Nobunaga was talking about. Kaku mentioned if Nobunaga stayed put at Kiyosu Castle, the most probable scenario he would be defeated and commit seppuku.[150]

This was not new in the Sengoku Era and it was the rule. (1) If one wanted to keep their holdings one must fight to keep them, (2) to protect them with an alliance, or (3) submit to some first-class power.[151] Nobunaga used the first method considering he had no other option and it was the only chance to succeed.

NOBUNAGA PREPARES FOR WAR 63

According to the *Shinchō-Kō ki*, Nobunaga laughed while one of his retainers tried to change his mind.[152] A retainer by the name of Hayashi Hidesada was completely at odds with Nobunaga. Hayashi knew the Oda army was no match for the Imagawa and tried to persuade Nobunaga to reconsider.[153] Hayashi was no fool. He wanted the clan to survive without the humiliation from the Imagawa. Hayashi was at Nobunaga's genpuku at Furuwatari Castle in 1546 and knew his father well. All he was doing was the better good for the Oda clan. In Yoshikawa Eiji's novel, *Taiko*, quoted Nobunaga speaking to Hayashi, "You're an old man…"[154] Nobunaga said it not as an insult to Hayashi, but spoke his opinion about the Imagawa advance. He knew the times were different from the past and new ideas were necessary to fight the enormous Imagawa army.

The outcome: Nobunaga went on his own true character, feelings, and did not depend on others for worthless advice. The result was to fight and die. Then he said, "It is late, return home!"[155] Everybody left the meeting after he spoke. Nobunaga's attitude towards Hayashi was arrogant and rude. What should be known he was a rare man who was ahead of his time. As a result, many of his subordinates and enemies never knew Nobunaga's true genius.

The question is was Nobunaga's decision to fight it out with Yoshimoto planned ahead of time? Yes, considering his mind made up long before any of senior advisers asked for tasteless advice. In fact, his advisers were bewildered since he was acting as if nothing has happened. He was not worried at all. He was playing mind games with his advisers and a key characteristic that made him a cut above the rest. If he started his campaign early in the morning, what did he do the rest of the night? Sleep. He knew the situation was uneasy; however, the most probable scenario would have been a nap here and there.

The next day Nobunaga was up at dawn and the first thing he did in the morning was to sing and dance to his favorite Nō play *Atsumori*, which runs:

Man's life is fifty years.

In the Universe what is it but dream and illusion?

Is there any who is born and does not die?[156]

Nobunaga allegedly held a fan in his hand. His lovely wife Nōhime played a hand drum.[157] His voice was low and grave and she was shedding tears while playing the hand drum.[158] The famous portrayal sounded romantic enough to make it authentic. Whether or not Nōhime was there during her husband's finest hour, one act was true. He was preparing for war and for his death.

Nobunaga loved songs, especially of *Kōwaka Atsumori* and was skilled novice of several arts.[159] There is theory that Nobunaga sang the verse three times before heading off to war.[160] The song and play itself related to the *Heike Monogatari*. In the movie *Kagemusha*, Nobunaga sang *Atsumori* just before receiving news about Takeda Katsuyori's attack on Nagashino Castle. While singing *Atsumori*, he was arranging himself for a crucial confrontation with death.

Nobunaga prepared for death and he prepared for it spiritually. Quoted in the *Shinchō-Kō ki* Nobunaga yelled,

"Blow the horn! Bring the armor!" (Horakai wo fuke! Bugu wo yokose!)[161] It must have been a restless and wild atmosphere at Kiyosu Castle with people mobilizing for war at the last minute. He put on his armor, had breakfast (consisted of rice gruel),[162] sounded the conch horn, and departed with a few men.

Then Nobunaga got on his horse "Tsukinowa" and departed.[163] According to Sugimoto Sonoko, the horse was chestnut colored and Nobunaga carried his "Honsho Masamune" sword with him to battle.[164] The few men he departed with were Iwamuro Nagato, Hasegawa Hashisuke, Sawaki Tōhachi (Maeda Toshiie's younger brother), Yamaguchi Hida, and Gatō Yasaburō.[165] The five men and their pages additionally journeyed along with Nobunaga.

Predominantly accepted is the men mentioned above rode with Nobunaga. However, according to the *Hoan Shinchōki*, more men journeyed with him early in the morning. The *Shinchōki* mentioned that Yanada Dewa no Kami along with three others went with him (Oda Miki no Jō, Kawajiri Hidetaka, and Sasa Uchi Zō no Suke).[166] If anybody stood out in Oze Hoan's *Shinchōki*, it would be Yanada Dewa no Kami (Masatsuna). He would provide Nobunaga with the chief intelligence that would win the battle. Owada Tetsuo did question the four men mentioned in the *Shinchōki* did not join Nobunaga early in the morning.[167] The most probable scenario would be Yanada and the three others did not join Nobunaga early in the morning, but arrived later during the day.

The Magic of Atsuta Shrine

Nobunaga marched further on and his fighting army slowly started to grow. He stopped at the distinguished Shinto shrine of Atsuta around eight o'clock in the morning.[168] Yoshikawa Eiji's novel, *Taiko*, quoted Nobunaga saying, "Even I am not going to go without saying a prayer."[169] This was meaningful considering he was not a deeply religious person. If anything he wanted at Atsuta was support for the battle he was about to fight. Kiyosu to Atsuta Shrine was roughly eight or nine miles (twelve kilometers).[170]

He wrote a prayer for victory and gave it to a retainer to deposit in a box at the shrine.[171] The letter or prayer allegedly abuses Yoshimoto as a bandit, a tyrant, and a butcher of Shintō shrines according to Sadler.[172] Intriguing enough Nobunaga would write evil acts about his enemies considering he would do something similar later on in life.

On his horse, he looked calm as ever, and humming to a tune. The priests were in awe and remarked, "He doesn't look a bit as if he just going into a fight."[173] Nobunaga continued to play his mind games considering he wanted to make a quick and daring attack on Yoshimoto. He had to act in a way to look as if he was not interested in fighting at all. When Nobunaga left the grounds of the shrine, he was riding his horse sitting sideways on his saddle with his hands on the front and back pommels.[174] The atmosphere at the shrine was perfect for him. He was at ease and fully relaxed. He told his troops at Atsuta, "The men are in armor and the sounds of the shell horn are of war, this is truly a good omen!"[175]

Things seemed bright for him at Atsuta even though the odds were against him. A story is often overlooked by historians is he created his own luck at Atsuta. For instance, it was said that Nobunaga grabbed some coins that were marked EiRaku Tsūhō. He threw them into the air as if it was a modern coin toss and all of the coins landed face up (heads).[176] Whether it was true or not, Nobunaga had luck on his side. Just before he departed, Nobunaga said if he triumphed, he would build a victory wall at the shrine.[177] The mud wall still exists today as a reminder of Nobunaga's triumph.

Nobunaga allegedly visited another shrine. According to the landmark, he made a stop at Hioki Shrine and prayed there. The shrine is still there today, but did he actually visited there is the question. Atsuta he visited; on the other hand, he might have made a brief call at Hioki too.

Atsuta proved to be a pivotal place since he was able to pick up more soldiers. Earlier I had mentioned bandits who joined the Oda army. Ronin who were on tough times could now seek the moment of glory since Nobunaga gave them an opportunity to do so. Not all the men who decided to join the Oda legion were bandits or ronin. He picked up stragglers and planned his attack ahead of time with the meager resources he had. If the numbers did not increase, the situation would have put Nobunaga in a desperate position. Attack the Imagawa or retreat. Nobunaga was confident he could defeat Yoshimoto. He was confident of a bloody victory or rotting in hell.

During the same time, Nobunaga was at Atsuta, Yoshimoto, and departed Kutsukake Castle around eight o'clock in the morning.[178] He was on his way to Ōdaka to pick up supplies and layout his final assault on Kiyosu. Heading west towards the Ōdaka path, Yoshimoto would take a brief rest at Okehazama, which later proved to be a fatal mistake. His scheduled plan to arrive at Ōdaka Castle in the early evening never fulfilled.

Ōdaka gave plenty of options for Yoshimoto. He could have taken the road from Narumi and use the Kamakura Ōkan that was the fastest way to Kiyosu.[179] With Marune and Washizu destroyed giving Yoshimoto a clear path to Ōdaka and Narumi. He would have some minor problems with Nakajima and Zenshōji. Fort Nakajima was near the Tōkaidō and Fort Zenshōji, which lies by the Kamakura Ōkan. The other alternative would be continuing to use the Tōkaidō from Okehazama and attack Fort Nakajima. Yoshimoto outnumbered all five forts and could have easily defeated them.

The last and interesting option was Ōdaka Castle a decoy. There is some speculation that Yoshimoto and his army went to Ōdaka to avoid a surprise attack. It would be hard to believe the theory considering the Imagawa advance was enormously quick. If it was true, Yoshimoto went to Ōdaka to avoid a surprise attack; then, it was a catastrophic mistake.

Fort Zenshōji and Nakajima

Nobunaga then took up a position opposite to the Imagawa camp at a place called Zenshōji very close to Narumi Castle on the Tōkaidō. There he displayed his banners and placed a fake army with dummy troops to make sure that his surprise attack against Imagawa would work.[180] Then he ordered Senshū Suetada and Sasa Masatsugu (Sasa Narimasa's older brother) along with three hundred men to attack Narumi.[181] The soldiers who attacked Narumi came from Sakuma Nobumori's army.[182]

Okabe Motonobu occupied Narumi Castle. Before he commanded the castle, one of Nobunaga's own, Yamaguchi Noritsugu held it. Noritsugu died in 1553, but before he passed away, it seemed the Yamaguchi family had some bad blood with the Oda. According to Jeroen Lamers, once Nobuhide died, the Yamaguchi family rebelled against the Oda (Battle of Akatsuka 1552). It was meaningful because Yoshimoto's home province of Suruga sent soldiers to raid Owari.[183] Nobunaga later forgave the Yamaguchi family and restored their landholdings.[184] Narumi was a key stronghold in Owari for Yoshimoto whereas it was a springboard to attack Kiyosu.

Zenshōji and the dummy troops did play role. Nobunaga might actually have left a thousand soldiers there.[185] One reason could be to cause distraction for Okabe Motonobu at Narumi. It would have bought just enough time for Nobunaga to locate Yoshimoto. If that was the case, he now had around two thousand soldiers instead of three thousand.

Why did Nobunaga attack Narumi? One answer could be a hit and run tactic. In return, Okabe Motonobu would have to defend Narumi more closely than usual to fend off future guerrilla attacks. He knew he did not have much to begin with, so three hundred were expendable for the operation. Two hundred and fifty soldiers did return and were able to fight at Okehazama. A small price paid for future glory. As mentioned earlier about the rigged army Nobunaga posted that could play a small factor. Since there was an attack on Narumi, another might have been possible. The rigged army could have been a diversion that prevented Okabe Motonobu to provide support in case of an emergency.

When Nobunaga arrived and departed from Zenshōji to Nakajima by crossing the Ōgi River (formerly known as the Kurosue River), he received some disturbing news. The news was about three hundred men he dispatched earlier to attack Narumi Castle.[186] Yoshimoto's men killed Sasa Masatsugu and Senshū Suetada along with fifty riders.[187] Noticed was Sasa Masatsugu's death whereas he served under Oda Nobuhide at the Battle of Azukisaka.[188]

Criticism still came from Nobunaga's superiors about the decision to go to Nakajima, which the Oda army arrived 12:00 M. The criticism was heading to Nakajima was suicide. For example, they quoted as saying:

Sir, the road there is flanked deep paddies. Once you step into them, you won't be able to move. Besides, you'll be forced to march in a single file. That will make the puny size of our forces perfectly visible to the enemy. This is out of the question, sir![189]

His superiors were not feeble-minded expressing their concerns about Nakajima. There were two problems. Nobunaga's mind already made up and determined to follow through at any cost. The other problem, Nakajima was the point of no return.

Yoshimoto had to be satisfied to hear that even a skimpy patrol could not harm his crusade to the capital. He additionally learned about Ieyasu and Asahina's victories at Marune and

Washizu around eleven o'clock in the morning.[190] This was significant since Yoshimoto learned the information before he stopped at Okehazama for lunch. In Yoshikawa's, *Taiko* quoted Yoshimoto as saying:

The heads of the Oda samurai from Narumi.

Line them up!

Let's take a look![191]

While inspecting the heads Yoshimoto knew Nobunaga was not about to give up without a fight. Looking at the heads, Yoshimoto said, "What a bloody mess!" and the head inspection was over.[192] He was brimming with confidence, which was important. Yoshimoto had the confidence that can to lead a victory over Nobunaga. Both men had the necessary confidence to lead their armies to glory.

There are various theories of Nobunaga's route to victory. For instance, in Owada's book, mapped out was Nobunaga route was Kiyosu, Atsuta, Zenshōji, Nakajima, and then Okehazama. The theory up to now was the same route, but with Nakajima omitted.[193]

On the other hand, Owada did have an opinion on the route Nobunaga took. In the *Shinchō-Kō ki*, omitted was the route extending from Nakajima.[194] The description in the Chronicle of the Battle of Okehazama differs (*Okehazama Kassenki*). It mentioned that Nobunaga's route was Nakajima, Aihara, Taishigane, and then Yoshimoto's camp.[195] Owada did not deny, but his opinion was after the rain, Nobunaga's army attacked the western part of

Okehazama.[196]   That meant Nobunaga's army attacked from the east and Yoshimoto marching west.

Lately, scholars have accepted Ōta Gyūichi's *Shinchō-Kō ki* more widely. It gives the author, Gyūichi, a chance to prove he was a true bibliographer and not a war propagandist. As stated earlier, the chances of him participating in the battle were high. The other theory has to be included to give the reader and scholar a balanced opinion and a chance to decide for themselves.

6

Yanada Masatsuna's Intelligence

FORT Washizu and Marune burnt to ashes and Nobunaga instead sent out scouts to find Yoshimoto. The report was that he was camped at a place called Dengaku-hazama, an area Nobunaga knew well since he roamed around the vicinity when he was a boy. Knowing the area where the battle will take place was significant and his country boy lifestyle was about to pay off. Yoshimoto had some rough knowledge of Owari domain because of the boundary castles between Owari/Mikawa borders, but not as well as Nobunaga.

In any event, the fool had the luxury of having the battle on his home turf. On his own intelligence, Nobunaga knew that Yoshimoto's forces lacked stable organization, and that if he could kill Yoshimoto, he could deal a deadly blow to his army.

How Nobunaga received, the information was a miracle from God. Yanada Masatsuna, the founding father of Sengoku human intelligence, was the individual who brought the data to Nobunaga.[197] Yanada also knew the area very well and he was a jizamurai or village samurai. Since he was a jizamurai, he must have known the geography's key components, and Nobunaga took full advantage of it.

The *Shinchō-Kō ki* had no mention of Yanada, but mainly accepted that he was the person who gave one of the most important pieces of data to Nobunaga. The opposite occurred in Oze Hoan's *Shinchōki,* where mentioned often was Yanada and was with Nobunaga right from the start; however, Owada stated earlier a different opinion. This makes sense since Yanada had to be in the border area (Owari-Mikawa) to spot Yoshimoto's main army.

As for Yanada Masatsuna, there is not much information about him. A tragedy since he would change Sengoku warfare history. On the other hand, his son, Yanada Hiromasa, has more data. Hiromasa served under Nobunaga and did well. He ended up governing Daisyōji Castle in Kaga (Ishikawa Prefecture) and passed away in 1579.

Nobunaga's use of intelligence needs more clarification since it was his greatest asset. He was far ahead of everybody else in the intelligence field during the Sengoku Era. Why was he far ahead of everybody else? The answer is simple. Intelligence was essential to survival! As a case in point, in the movie *Kagemusha*, Nobunaga was furious when the intelligence he received on the death of Takeda Shingen was vague. He wanted the truth now and hated delays. To receive the information he had to push his spies to the brink or it was death to the clan.

At Fort Nakajima, Yanada said, "Yoshimoto and his army are taking a break at Dengakuhazama." Nobunaga replied, "Is that so, they entered Dengakuhazama."[198] Yanada's information was the key component for Nobunaga's decision to attack Yoshimoto quickly and was one of the turning points of the battle.

Time was critical. If Nobunaga did not act fast to Yanada's intelligence, the chances of him succeeding surely greatly decreased. He was able to act quickly on the intelligence seeing Yanada had no bureaucratic chain of command. Yanada went straight to Nobunaga and reported Yoshimoto's camp location. Nobunaga's senior retainers were so restrained they tried to persuade him to think again. He would have none of it and went on his true character and feelings.

Nobunaga replied, "Last night the forts of Washizu and Marune were taken, supplies were brought to Ōdaka; still the enemy must be tired."[199] One has to remember that it was not Yoshimoto's main army, but his allied army of the Matsudaira and the Ii families who did most of work the previous night. The thinking of Nobunaga's retainers did not fit the times to fight the rapidly changing Sengoku warfare.

In the end, Nobunaga's superiors would be the real losers. Hayashi Hidesada, who questioned Nobunaga's decision to fight it out the night before the battle, again doubted the decision to continue to fight.[200] If the Oda clan was on its last leg, Hayashi was going to be a part of it. Nobunaga's army arrived at the outskirts of Okehazama around one o'clock in the afternoon waiting for the perfect opportunity to attack.

Nobunaga was keen enough to know the situation of the Imagawa army. He knew the Imagawa army was active and needed to take a break. The break would be enough time for him to plan an all out attack to squash the Imagawa. The other side would be the Yoshimoto's army needed a recess to allow the rest of the army to catch up. For instance, supplies lines could arrive from the backside. Yoshimoto's main army needed the rest; however, it was brief. The day of the battle, the weather was extremely hot. The army and Yoshimoto himself were exhausted from the intense heat. Unfortunately, caught off guard was Yoshimoto.

After Yoshimoto inspected the heads there was a huge victory party with food, sake, Nō songs chanted, and even the possibility of a tea ceremony at camp.[201] A case in point, a daisu (a utensil stand) was at the party.[202] As for the chakai, there are no remaining documents, although suspected the chances were high there was one due to Yoshimoto's attachment to high culture.

Buddhist monks and Shintō priests in the area around Okehazama provided food and sake. According to the Chōfukuji landmark, the head priest Zenku received Yoshimoto and provided the army with food and drink. During the party, Yoshimoto was in a surcoat of red brocade, armor with a white breastplate, a sword by Samonji, and a dagger by Matsukura Gō, as he sat viewing the heads of his defeat enemies.[203]

There were several reasons why the monks and priests provided provisions. One was fear. Yoshimoto might punish the monks and priests for aiding Nobunaga. Second, if Yoshimoto was clever enough to use the people for future use if he defeated Nobunaga. As a case in point, in Yoshikawa Eiji's, *Taiko*, Yoshimoto stated, "We'll reward them when we return from the capital."[204] It was still daylight and Yoshimoto took it for granted that neither God nor the Devil dare to meet his armies.[205] The wrath of Nobunaga was about to eradicate Yoshimoto's victory party.

Nobunaga's Secret Weapon: The Thunderstorm

The afternoon sky became black and a violent rainstorm stabilized Yoshimoto's troops. The rain that came down that day was not an ordinary storm. It was downright deadly and wicked. Noted in the *Shinchō-Kō ki*, Nobunaga and his troops said the storm was so violent, it wondered if Atsuta Shrine started its own battle.[206] This was favorable for Nobunaga and it was by chance the thunderclouds came whereas it forced Yoshimoto's army to hunker under the trees.[207]

If anything came out positive for Yoshimoto's men about the barrage, it cooled the army from the intense heat. The day of the battle was terribly hot. How important was the thunderstorm? According to Owada Tetsuo, the violent thunderstorm was one the deciding factors in the battle. He then pointed out the Imagawa scout party were either negligent or could not see the Oda approach because of the heavy rain.[208]

When the thunderstorm started is another question. Yoshimoto stopped at Okehazama around noon. If the battle started around two o'clock in the afternoon; then, the rain started between 12:00 M. and 2:00 P.M. Owada Tetsuo mentioned in his book, *Okehazama no Tatakai*, that the rain started while Yoshimoto's troops were eating or just finished eating their lunch.[209] Nobody knows for sure when the rain began; however, it might have started while finishing up on lunch.

In the end, the thunderstorm was Nobunaga's best

friend and secret weapon. A weapon he fully took advantage.
The thunderstorm, which forced Yoshimoto's troops to huddle
together, made them easy targets. If there were no thunderstorm,
Yoshimoto's troops most likely be spread out and could spot
Nobunaga. If the weather did change, so will the result.

Nobunaga offered words of encouragement to his army.
He reminded them what was at stake and, if they win the battle,
they will be heroes of Owari.

If the enemy attacks, retreat. If he retreats, give chase.
Don't capture anybody. Just leave him alone. If we win in this
battle, those taking part will bring honor to your houses, your
reputation assured in generations to come.[210]

He told his men if it was the other way around, by all means
retreat. Nobunaga was no fool and he had to strike first blood or
it was over for the Oda. Whether or not Nobunaga said it to his
troops, he knew history was in the making. History he wanted to
share with his troops. Concisely, his charisma rubbed off on his
soldiers.

At the same time, some of Nobunaga's warriors returned
from the Narumi Castle raid with enemy heads. These soldiers
included Maeda Toshiie, Mōri Kawachi, Mori Juburō, Kinoshita
Uta no Suke, Nakagawa Kinemon, Sakuma Yatarō, Mori Kosuke,
Ajiki Yatarō, and Uozumi Hayato.[211] Nobunaga's finest hour was
about come.

7

Yoshimoto's Death

THE lethal rain finally stopped and the black clouds blown away by the wind, and by 2:00 P.M., it was time for Nobunaga to make his quick deadly attack on Imagawa Yoshimoto. He cried out:

Now is the time to attack the enemy. This is a good opportunity to distinguish yourselves in battle. Seek only Yoshimoto; ignore all others.[212]

He made his small army's job simple by designating Yoshimoto as the key target. Focusing on Yoshimoto than the others was easier than trying to smash the entire Imagawa army. The on the field decision by Nobunaga was pure genetic genius. Only God could have given that talent to him. After giving the final orders, Nobunaga with a spear in his hand led the attack. Nobunaga yelled, "Kakare! Kakare!"[213] Then the Oda troops attacked with vigor. Yoshimoto's victory party was about to be crushed.

How Nobunaga spotted Yoshimoto was by sheer luck.

When Yoshimoto departed from his Sunpu headquarters, he took a lacquered palanquin (koshi) with him.[214] Why did Yoshimoto use a palanquin in the first place? In Owada's *Imagawa Yoshimoto*, he explained Yoshimoto's unfit physical appearance, but most likely a Muromachi Shogun house custom.[215] The palanquin had to be near Yoshimoto and if it was, made Nobunaga's task easier to find him.[216] Worse yet, weapons (guns, spears, and bows) for the Imagawa army were stuck in the mud due to the rain, which meant they were unprepared to counter the ambush.

How many troops rested with Yoshimoto at Okehazama? Yoshimoto did bring about 25,000, but they all did not rest with him at Okehazama. Most of the soldiers departed earlier in the campaign. *Mō Hitosu no Okehazama* listed approximately 6,000 soldiers.[217] Owada listed 5,000 troops.[218] The most probable scenario Yoshimoto had approximately around 5,000-6,000 soldiers. However, Yoshimoto had trouble with Nobunaga by the surprise attack.

Caught off guard by the quick ambush was Yoshimoto. Nobunaga's army blitzed through the enemy with direct hits. The entire Imagawa camp was in a total state of chaos and left Yoshimoto unprotected. Protected only with a sparse unit of three hundred men, this quickly reduced to fifty.[219] Even if he had proper protection, it did not matter.

Yoshimoto's days numbered after his soldiers evaporated since Nobunaga's attack was too quick. Then Nobunaga's samurai and ashigaru units approached with the intent to kill. Yoshimoto knew very well that he was in deep trouble. Death was near and had no choice but to fight.

At first Yoshimoto, thought there was a drunken brawl from his troops and told them to be quiet.[220] The drunken brawl that did not happen needs to be illustrated. He stopped at Okehazama to rest and had some lunch. The last thing he needed was his men intoxicated. Drunken soldiers would have been a disaster since Yoshimoto's plan was to meet Ieyasu at Ōdaka. Undisciplined men never won battles or wars. They created problems instead of solving them. Sake was the standard drink, but he knew during lunch the intake of alcohol had to be limited. The alcohol was restricted considering the day's work was never finished. In Yoshikawa Eiji's, *Taiko* mentioned that the alcohol was limited since the objective was Ōdaka Castle.[221]

Nobunaga himself had the opportunity to get into the action. The *Shinchō-Kō ki* made it clear that during the battle Nobunaga got off his horse and fought the Imagawa army. He was fighting side by side with his foot soldiers that were young and brave.

During this event, Nobunaga showed his strong leadership by example. He was able to show his true character: a Soldier of Fortune with samurai spirit. He fought along with his men during a time of crisis and he was able to earn his trust with his troops giving emotional support. Soon Nobunaga's brave valor would spread throughout the country.

As the battle worn on, Yoshimoto withdrew his sword and cut through the shaft of a spear. The incision was so deep that it made a bloody gash on the assailant's knee. Hattori Haruyasu unfortunately received the harsh blow. Yoshikawa described the wound as "...split open like a pomegranate..."[222] Then a second came and took Yoshimoto's head as a victory prize for

Nobunaga. Mōri Shinsuke received credit in taking Yoshimoto's head (killed along with Nobunaga in 1582 at the Honnōji Rebellion in Kyoto).[223] A prize that was highly valued during the Sengoku Era.

Mōri Shinsuke's job was not smooth. He paid the price for victory when he lost his finger. During the skirmish, Shinsuke's finger managed to slide into Yoshimoto's mouth. Knowing death was only seconds away Yoshimoto gnawed off Shinsuke's finger.[224] Never forgotten, is Hattori Haruyasu whereas he ended up preventing Yoshimoto an opportunity to escape while giving Shinsuke a chance to take Yoshimoto's head.

The rest of Imagawa army was trying to escape through wet rice paddies and Nobunaga's army unmercifully cut many down. Two of Yoshimoto's (Shimada Sakyō and Sawada Nagato no Kami) men went to their horses and try to flee, but were chased down and butchered.[225] Nobunaga's lower class soldiers now had the opportunity for glory by taking the heads of the fleeing Imagawa army. He had to be pleased with joy his men slaughtered the enemy with great success. The time was approximately 4:00 P.M. when the battle was completed.[226] Unfortunately, Gyūichi did not write down what time the conflict was finished.

Yoshimoto was forty-two years old when killed in action. For a man who was better at the arts and luxury in life, he died a soldier. Nobunaga and his army cried shouts of victory after the hard fought bloody conquest. A victory would make his father, Nobuhide, proud since he had trouble with Yoshimoto in the past. It took years for Nobuhide to fend off the Imagawa, yet his son did it in a single stroke. One other person had to be impressed,

Hayashi Hidesada, the man who was against Nobunaga from the start. He must have felt relieved the Oda was safe for the time being.

Nobunaga returned to Kiyosu Castle where he would be welcomed as a hero from the people of Owari and the town of Kiyosu. Before arriving, he went to pay a return visit to the Atsuta Shrine to show the Shintō priests his new booty.

According to the *Okehazama Kassenki*, Nobunaga rode in to shrine grounds with Yoshimoto's head to the left of the saddle.[227] A mob of people consisting families of the priests came to see what Nobunaga brought. They had to be in complete shock! This same person acted as if he was not going into battle. The crowd were completely surprised by the fact Nobunaga actually defeated the mighty Imagawa. Nobunaga presented a sacred horse to the shrine as a gift of conquest. If the gift was true, it was a reward to the Gods at Atsuta for blessing Nobunaga's victory. At the shrine, prayers of victory chanted, and afterward by dusk, he returned to Kiyosu[228].

The result was the unexpected from Nobunaga. Society who still had doubts that Nobunaga was an idiot now had a second opinion about the man. If the prayer earlier in the morning promised victory by Nobunaga was true in heart; then, the war gods accepted it.

Nobunaga's returning to Atsuta Shrine was more detailed in the *Okehazama Kassenki* then the *Shinchō-Kō ki*. It was a historic event returning to Atsuta; however, the main reason why he was returning there was to prove he was no longer a fool and he wanted respect seriously.

When Nobunaga finally arrived at Kiyosu in the evening,

the town gave him a hero's welcome. He spoke to the people of Kiyosu with energy and passion. In Yoshikawa Eiji's novel, *Taiko*, Nobunaga spoke with passion:

Take a look at the head of the great lord of the Imagawa! This is the souvenir I have brought back to you. From tomorrow on, the troubles at the border will be over. Be diligent and work hard. Work hard and enjoy yourselves![229]

What Nobunaga was trying to say to the people of Kiyosu the problem with the Imagawa was finished.

Head Inspection

Nobunaga summoned a firm inspection of the decapitated heads at Kiyosu Castle and was extremely joyous that his ultimate prize for glory, Imagawa Yoshimoto's head was his at last. He knew the kubijiken (head viewing ceremony) was about to come up was extremely rare. Over 3,000 decapitated heads taken in the battle including 500 officers and men.[230] As a case in point, Owada stated in his book, *Okehazama no Tatakai*, that the *Butokuhennenshūsei* listed 583 bushi and 2,500 others killed.[231] It meant 583 samurai and 2,500 ashigaru were killed in action.

Besides taking Yoshimoto's head Nobunaga took his sword as a prize too. The sword (Samonji) is now located at Takeisao Shrine (also known as Kenkun Jinja) in Kyoto. The shrine also includes armor worn by Nobunaga and a copy of Ōta Gyūichi's *Shinchō-Kō ki*. Yoshimoto acquired the sword when he married Takeda Nobutora's daughter. Nobutora obtained it

from Miyoshi Nagamasa (Sōzan). According to Owada Tetsuo's
Okehazama no Tatakai, Tokugawa Ieyasu received the sword as
well.[232]

    A Buddhist priest by the name, Kaiō, who worked
at the Songenji Temple, buried the dead and did a memorial
service for them (place known as Senninzuka).[233] Battle
casualties were high. According to Turnbull, sixty-two named
samurai who present with Yoshimoto at Okehazama all but two
slain.[234] Turnbull's reference came from Hayashi Ryosho's,
Okehazama no Tatakai. He further noted Nobunaga's samurai,
which was around sixty, and out of those sixty, six slain in
battle. Unfortunately, Turnbull did not have any of the names
listed killed in action except for Yoshimoto. Owada Tetsuo's
Okehazama no Tatakai and Naramoto Tatsuya's *Sengoku Bushō
Monoshiri Jiten* did list several of the killed in action on both
sides.

    For example, the *Sengoku Bushō Monoshiri Jiten*
listed the main men lost (Azai Masatoshi, Ii Naomori, and Inō
Noritsura).[235] Owada written two pages which consisted the
main loyal retainers who were killed at the Battle of Okehazama
(Yoshida Ujiyoshi, Yamada Shinzaemon, Okabe Nagasada,
Sekiguchi Chikamasa, Ihara Mimasaka no Kami, Muira
Yoshinari, Tominaga Hōki, Saitō Kamon no Suke, Asahina
Kazue no Suke Hideaki, Katsuyama Harima no Kami Nagayoshi,
and Matsui Munenobu).[236] Matsui Munenobu (forty-six years
old when killed) was the lord of Futamata Castle in Tōtōmi. The
present location in Toyoake City, in the hills of Kōtokuin Temple
(Shingon sect), has a memorial stone on his death at Okehazama.

    Killed in action was Ii Naomori, one of the two allied

families who led main body of troops on the 10th at the age of fifty-five. The Ii family was famous during the late Sengoku Era (Ii Naomasa, who participated in the Battle of Sekigahara 1600, his father was Ii Naochika). Naomori was fighting at Fort Washizu during the Okehazama prelude. One possibility might be he left Fort Washizu to inform Yoshimoto about victories at Fort Marune and Washizu.

The *Shinchō-Kō ki* did not have any mention how many men were lost at Okehazama except for the kubijiken (head viewing ceremony). The Oda army lost around a thousand soldiers.[237] A high casualty rate considering Nobunaga brought two thousand directly to the battlefield. Killed were numerous of his young ashigaru and pages who served who fought with him in battle. He had no other choice but to pay the price for glory. The paid expense was in blood, nevertheless the victory prize made it all too rewarding. He knew he was going to suffer casualties small or large, but his goal was to kill Yoshimoto. Okehazama's dead on both sides totaled approximately around four thousand.

Yoshimoto's head was another story. After the inspection of the decapitated heads at Kiyosu, Yoshimoto's head returned to his headquarters in Sunpu. Sources such as *Mikawa Monogatari*, *Shinchō-Kō ki*, and *Okehazama no Tatakai* all have something noted about it.

The individual responsible for bringing back Yoshimoto's head to Sunpu was Okabe Motonobu (who would serve under the Takeda clan after the fall of the Imagawa), who was guarding Narumi Castle.[238] Motonobu was stubborn at first since he refused to surrender to Nobunaga. He was impressed with

Motonobu, but he knew Motonobu was no longer a threat to him. Then Nobunaga said, "It is admirable of Okabe to continue to defend the castle even though he is surrounded by the enemy."[239] If anything came out of the meeting between Nobunaga, Motonobu there was no further, and unnecessary bloodshed. As for Narumi, the castle demolished sometime after 1573.

Motonobu along with ten Buddhist priests and his army went back to Sunpu with Yoshimoto's head.[240] Later Motonobu attacked Kariya Castle, which Mizuno Nobuchika held at the time being.[241] It was a lost cause and the remaining Imagawa army killed Nobuchika.[242]

Why did Okabe Motonobu attack Kariya? One theory could be to make up for the heavy Okehazama defeat. Another reason could be the Mizuno were an ally of the Oda. Ieyasu's mother, Ōdai, came from Kariya. Yoshimoto's pacifist son, Ujizane, was certainly cheerful about Okabe Motonobu's success at Kariya.

A head of a famous general or samurai was a precious prize during the Sengoku Era. Without a doubt, Nobunaga made a drastic mistake by allowing Yoshimoto's head to return to Sunpu. A treasure that valuable whould have been coveted by Nobunaga and should be used as a warning to all when trying to invade Owari. Psychology was only part of the battle and it was important. If Nobunaga wanted a psychological advantage; then, he should kept the head as a trophy.

On the other hand, if he wanted precaution against the Imagawa clan; then, it was a wise decision to return Yoshimoto's head. Walter Dening's, *The Life of Toyotomi Hideyoshi*, quoted young Hideyoshi talking about returning Yoshimoto's head to prevent further action.[243]

The Rinzaiji Temple which still stands today in
Shizuoka City is now the modern day mausoleum for Imagawa
Yoshimoto.[244] Where Yoshimoto rests is another story. It is
highly possible that Yoshimoto's buried body is at Daisyōji
in Aichi Prefecture, Ushikubo Town.[245] An excavation at the
temple ground can prove he rests there, but now there has
been no excavation done and only speculation he was inhumed
at Daisyōji.[246] Three years (1563) later after the Battle of
Okehazama, Ujizane performed a memorial service there.

Nobunaga did one positive gesture towards the death of
Yoshimoto. It was noted in the *Shinchō-Kō ki* he ordered a giant
sotoba, (a wooden grave tablet), to be built south of Kiyosu near
Atsuta at Sukaguchi (Shinkawa Town, Aichi Prefecture).[247]

Okehazama Battlefield

Where Yoshimoto killed and the battleground itself was
and still is a great story. Accepted generally, is that Okehazama
is the place where Yoshimoto perished. There are two historical
landmarks dedicated to the Battle of Okehazama. The first
landmark is located at Toyoake City, Sakae-chō in Aichi
Prefecture. Toyoake City's location received official status in
1937.[248] As for who gave the status, the Ministry of Education
did it. Many landmarks related to the battle are located there.
For example, Yoshimoto's camp, the memorial for the dead, the
seven pillars are the tombs of Yoshimoto's generals, and a stone
where Yoshimoto killed. Included were a stone for Yamada
Shinzaemon and the pages. Hitomi (1729-1797) built them in

the eighth year of Meiwa, 18 December 1771. That same day and year, constructed was Matsui Munenobu's tomb.

The second one is located at Midori-ku, Arimatsu-chō also in Aichi Prefecture. According to Owada Tetsuo, Yoshimoto made his last stand at the second location at Dengakutsubō kosenjō in Arimatsu.[249] Stephen Turnbull's, *Battles of the Samurai*, again noted the Arimatsu location was the place where Yoshimoto killed.[250] Turnbull rarely or did not mentioned the Toyoake City location at all. There is a water well where the Oda soldiers cleaned Yoshimoto's decapitated head. Additional landmarks include the Senpyo-no-Matsu or the War Council Pine Tree. The landmark is where an Imagawa general, Sena Ujitoshi, gathered his men at the tree. If there were a case for the Arimatsu location, it would be the Chōfukuji Temple (Seizan sect of Jōdo Buddhism). Stated earlier, the priest of the temple provided refreshments to Yoshimoto and his legion.

Owada Tetsuo further noted in his book, *Okehazama no Tatakai*, the Toyoake City landmark is related, and did have some significance related to the battle.[251] This was an influential statement by Owada whereas both sites joined as one. His opinion could be valid as both landmarks are almost approximately less than two miles southwest from each other (approximately one kilometer apart).

The appointment of the historical landmark in Toyoake City, Sakae-chō was without a doubt political. As a case in point, Owada Tetsuo explained influential politicians had something to do with the decision.[252] Both landmarks are located near a temple, which is remarkable. For instance, Toyoake City's landmark is located near Kōtokuin and Arimatsu-chō's is located near Chōfukuji.

To make Midori-ku, Arimatsu-chō's case worse is the location. Toyoake City location is enormously close to the Meitetsu train station; however, the Arimatsu location is difficult and too far for the traveler to find. According to Togawa Jun, this is the main problem why very few people visit or even know the site.[253]

As for a conclusion, special interest groups who wanted Toyoake City as the official Battlefield of Okehazama politically pushed the 1937 decision. Was it important? As stated earlier, both places played key roles and marked as historical battlegrounds. Second, the city had to make a decision. The masses wanted a recognized historical landmark. Both Okehazama landmarks are valid and treated as such.

The most significant event happened at Okehazama was the death of Yoshimoto, since there was nobody who could rally the army. Once he killed, confidence was quickly lost and chaos erupted. Something Nobunaga wanted in the first place. Two people in mind, Okabe Motonobu (Narumi Castle) and Asahina Yasutomo (likely returned to Ōdaka Castle after the raid on Washizu) were not at Okehazama. Both Motonobu and Yasutomo were adequate; however, the loss of Yoshimoto proved too chaotic for any of the two to take charge and regroup. If Yoshimoto escaped death at the Battle of Okehazama; thus, the result would have been certainly different and Nobunaga's situation would have been too.

8

The What If Scenario

IF Yoshimoto triumphed at the Battle of Okehazama; then, he would have taken over Owari with hardly any resistance at all. After Owari would be Mino. Saitō Yoshitatsu governed the province. Yoshimoto would have arrived in Kyoto with intentions only imaginable. If he did claim Kyoto, there would be some heavy issues to deal with. One would be the thirteenth Ashikaga shogun Yoshiteru. Other families Yoshimoto would have to administer with besides the Saitō were, the Asakura clan in Echizen (present day Fukui), the Azai clan in Ōmi (Shiga Prefecture), the Rokkaku (southern Ōmi), and the Mōri clan (western Honshu).

Yoshimoto would have to administer with these families to establish his grip in Japan. His diplomacy skills were superb. However, can he fight his way out if diplomacy fails? Who knows? Nobunaga later on in his career had to deal with the same problems mentioned above.

The shogun situation has to be illustrated. Kaku Kōzō's book, *Oda Nobunaga Zen Shigoto*, noted that Yoshimoto had the chance to rebuild the Ashikaga Bakufu.[254] This is significant whereas he might have had the opportunity to play a vast role in Kyoto politically and militarily. The Imagawa did have a relationship with the Ashikaga government in the past and it might have been a blessing for Yoshiteru if Yoshimoto arrived in the city he loved. If all mentioned above failed, Yoshimoto would have the probability to create his own government in his name.

The question is what if Nobunaga and Yoshimoto both survived the battle. Clearly would have been in Yoshimoto's favor. He had more troops, resources, and allies than Nobunaga. Earlier noted if Nobunaga had stayed at Kiyosu Castle, he would have killed himself. Yoshimoto would have the time to learn from his Okehazama blunder and prevent a future surprise attack. A peace pact with Nobunaga would have been puzzling and rare, nevertheless, could have been a possibility. If a truce were going to occur Yoshimoto would need a skilled leader and negotiator after his mentor Sūfu passed away in 1555. If Yoshimoto were going to make a second attempt at Kyoto, he would have to think carefully the next time around. Nobunaga was no pushover.

Continuing with a Yoshimoto victory, Owari would have been a great prize for him. Rivers that flow into Ise Bay were important for shipping and travel. It would have produced large sums of revenue for him. Atsuta and Tsushima ports were rich and necessary for the success of Owari. The income would have been a boost for Yoshimoto's lavish lifestyle. Trade, but more important, fertile land for farming, and it would have made Yoshimoto's crusade to Kyoto much smoother. Owari was only a short hop to Mino. Whoever governed Mino, their chances to control Japan vastly increased.

Last was the Oda house. What would happen if Nobunaga defeated? The presumptive scenario would be the total collapse of the Oda house. He just brought the Oda house in order only one year earlier. Who would replace Nobunaga as the heir? Nobutada was only a baby and Nobunaga's uncles who joined him after unifying Owari were decent, yet did not have his charisma. This would a major problem; however, Nobunaga triumphed. The house issue went to the Imagawa. Even though the Imagawa house was more stable than the Oda, Yoshimoto was in power for years; however, reality proved a different story. It crumbled after Yoshimoto's death.

Nobunaga was clearly the big winner of the battle. He knew the odds were very slim. How bold, daring, and downright dangerous was his surprise attack? If Nobunaga gave any hint that he was planning to make a quick hit and run attack on the Imagawa forces; thus, routed the army easily because he simply did not have enough troops to do the job. As mentioned before, the rain was a key factor, but also Nobunaga's quick blitzkrieg assault. If anything needed to prove, it was Nobunaga's opinion from his critics. He was no longer an idiot and was a person earnestly taken.

Worse yet, where was Ieyasu? Was he supposed to lead a secondary front? Earlier mentioned he stopped, rested, and was able to meet his mother at Akoi Castle in Owari. It was only fitting luck was on Nobunaga's side. When Ieyasu heard the news about Yoshimoto's sudden death, he was shocked. He could not believe his lord perished in action. Now he had a reason not to withdraw from Ōdaka. "because if the news should be false, and Yoshimoto still alive, it would not look at all well."[255] Yoshimoto expected to arrive at Ōdaka around four in the afternoon. He was expecting his lord to arrive at Ōdaka, which never happened.

Ieyasu's uncle, Nobumoto of Kariya who had some common sense to persuade Ieyasu to withdraw.[256] Nobumoto was wise. He was concerned because Nobunaga might take the chance to attack. Ieyasu departed to Okazaki on the same night of Yoshimoto's death instead of his former lord's domain. He could not return directly to Okazaki for the reason that Imagawa soldiers were still occupying Okazaki Castle or close by. If he did, the remaining Imagawa army would be suspicious of him. On the twentieth, he departed Chiryū and continued on his way back, but he stopped at Daijuji Temple until the Imagawa troops left Okazaki Castle.[257] At the temple it was written in Stephen Turnbull's book, *Japanese Warrior Monks AD 949-1603*, Ieyasu was about to commit seppuku, but the chief priest persuaded him not to do it.[258] It would be odd if he would actually kill himself. After all, Yoshimoto treated the Matsudaira clan poorly.

It was not until the twenty-third Ieyasu was able to return to Okazaki.[259] He must have felt relieved that he was able to return safely home without fighting Nobunaga, who without a doubt must have been enormously confident.

Yoshimoto's Weakness

Yoshimoto had a lot going against him. Much of the blame has to go to himself. As a case in point, alcohol and arrogance were the deadly twin evils that haunted Imagawa Yoshimoto.[260] The Imagawa clan treated Ieyasu and his family like dirt. According to

Sadler, he purposely spared his men as much as possible and used the men of Mikawa instead on campaigns.[261] Sparing his men was a disaster whereas they were not battle seasoned. The glory went to the allied army, not Yoshimoto's main army. Ieyasu's men along with the help of the Ii did much of the early fighting and it was the primary reason why Yoshimoto had early success at Okehazama.[262]

He was not a popular person after his death. It is not difficult to find out why. Robbed were Mikawa's revenue and used by Imagawa with hardly anything remaining.[263] The money Yoshimoto took no doubt used for his luxurious living and building projects. The way Sadler pictured Imagawa Yoshimoto as an evil villain who took full advantage of Ieyasu and the men of Mikawa. When Ieyasu had to make a choice between the Imagawa and the Oda, it had to be a simple decision to make.

If bad luck or an evil omen haunted Yoshimoto, it was his number of succession. He was the ninth heir to the Imagawa clan.[264] The number nine considered an unlucky number in Japanese society. For example, the number thirteen considered an unlucky number in the United States. If that was the case, Yoshimoto was doomed at the start. His son Ujizane was the tenth in line of the Imagawa family. Yoshimoto bequeath the clan to his son in 1557; however, he was no natural leader. Ujizane's fame to claim was he survived the chaos. Stephen Turnbull who said, "A born loser he may have been, but Ujizane was one of nature's survivors."[265]

Another deciding factor was the death of Yoshimoto's mentor Sūfu. He taught Yoshimoto war strategy, government, and administration. His death five years earlier had no direct impact on the battle. If Yoshimoto wanted sound advice on Okehazama, he could not get it. This was important considering Sūfu was almost a high-ranking general for the Imagawa army. He also lost Sūfu's diplomatic and leadership skills as well. If he was still around by the time of the battle, the result might have been different, the campaign might have never occurred, or the mass disarray occurred during and after the battle might not be as destructive. At the end, Yoshimoto did not use his learned skills from his teacher and it cost him his life and the clan.

Young Ieyasu was a good replacement, and rapidly growing into a fine warrior; however, he was still green. More important, he did not have Sūfu's experience. Ieyasu learned from Sūfu at Rinzaiji in Sunpu who proved to be a fantastic teacher, but that was during his younger days.

If one wanted to argue that Nobunaga lost Hirate Masahide in 1553 to balance Yoshimoto's loss of Sūfu was equal, yet they had different consequences. Nobunaga learned from his mistake of mocking his senior adviser and overcame it. More important, he was a self-made man. Yoshimoto did not learn from his mishaps and it showed during his military campaigns. The result proved Yoshimoto still had to rely on others for military strategy considering he was an ordinary soldier.

The other factor was why going to Ōdaka in the first place. Yoshimoto could have sent someone to send supplies or a message to Ieyasu. If Yoshimoto was so concerned to arrive in Kyoto quickly as possible, he should have marched to Narumi by taking the Kamakura Ōkan or the Tōkaidō. Okabe Motonobu could have supplied Yoshimoto anything he needed. Narumi would have provided a chance to take Kiyosu by taking the Kamakura Ōkan and occupying Kiyosu would have made the road to Kyoto quicker.

Earlier referred that Fort Zenshōji, just west of the Kamakura Ōkan, built by Nobunaga, and left about a thousand men, yet Okabe Motonobu easily outnumbered them even with reinforcements. Even with Fort Nakajima lying on the Ōgi River and the Tōkaidō, Yoshimoto still had the resources to overcome both forts. Heading northwest and resting at Okehazama proved to be fatal.

Yoshimoto might not have been physically ready to fight. In Yoshikawa's, *Taiko*, Yoshimoto was fat and it was due to his opulent lifestyle.[266] Additionally noted it was an ordeal for him to go on such a campaign to begin with.[267] In Owada Tetsuo's *Imagawa Yoshimoto*, Yoshimoto was too fat and could not ride a horse.[268] If it was true Yoshimoto was overweight, all the culpability goes to him for not physically prepared for a long war campaign. Worse yet, Tokugawa Ieyasu's biographer, A.L. Sadler called Yoshimoto a "little lame man."[269] Who was at best, supposed to be a patron of the arts. Nobunaga was quite the opposite. He was slim, slender, and physically fit for battle. His fitness is simple to interpret. It was due to his Owari country lifestyle.

An eerie moment occurred just when Yoshimoto departed for Kyoto. In Owada's *Okehazama no Tatakai*, a woman who was area of the Imagawa palace was chanting in a sad and depressing voice.[270] It was obvious the woman was worried about him. Her inner feelings: Yoshimoto's time on earth was up. The woman's

voice did not play a role, but her expression of concern could have
been an evil omen for Yoshimoto's Kyoto campaign.

Yoshimoto cursed at the start. There was even the ghost
of his illegitimate brother Genkōetan.[271] The supposed ghost did
not bring any good news to Yoshimoto at all. In fact, the ghost
was an evil omen meant his chances of surviving the battle were
slim. It was bizarre. Yet seriously taken in Sengoku Japan was
superstitions and the like. The reverse occurred when Nobunaga
threw the EiRaku Tsūhō coins at Atsuta Shrine where he created
his own fate and luck.

Last was Kyoto. Earlier mentioned Yoshimoto was
fanatical about Kyoto. Many Sengoku daimyo had the same goal
to occupy the capital. Numerous were killed trying and some
never had the chance during their lifetime. Backstabbing was the
norm in Sengoku Japan; thus, Nobunaga and Yoshimoto had their
share. Yoshimoto spent time in Kyoto that it felt like home. Only
problem: he could not rule Sengoku Japan. Nobunaga would have
much more success in the capital than Yoshimoto ever dreamed.
Kyoto would be one of main the factors of his death. He was too
rabid about the capital. Eight years later, Nobunaga along with
Ashikaga Yoshiaki would march into the streets of Kyoto. Berry
concluded the Imagawa weakness, "Among the most innovative
of administrators, the Imagawa proved able in defense but weak
in offensive strategy."[272]

The Four Key Points

The rainstorm, intelligence from Yanada Masatsuna, Nobunaga's small army, and Okehazama itself were the four key turning points of the battle. Without them, the possibilities of success would have been slim or none.

Pointed out earlier, Owada Tetsuo said the rain was one of the deciding components in the battle (negligence or could not see Nobunaga's troops due to the rain). He was correct. The rain was unpredictable and no way to prevent it. One has to remember that the rainstorm was so violent to the point both sides were scared, and it was obvious Yoshimoto's army was frightened from the storm. There was no modern technology back then to predict when and where rain would fall.

The rain forced Yoshimoto's army to look for cover, which meant they were less prepared for battle. Rain made Nobunaga's army less detectable (dark skies). Noted earlier, bows, guns, and spears were stuck in the mud made it harder to fight. Nobunaga took full advantage of Yoshimoto's mishaps, which cost him his life. Defeating Yoshimoto without modern technology made the victory even more remarkable. One author quoted as saying Nobunaga was the "rainy season shogun!"[273]

A way to prevent Yanada Masatsuna's intelligence access was by scouting the area that surrounded Okehazama. The information Nobunaga received from Yanada was just as important as the rain since he knew the vicinity. Since Yanada was a jizamurai, he knew the area handily, and made Nobunaga's job easier. However, Yoshimoto blew his chance for Kyoto because he personally did not know the border area genuinely well.

On the contrary, according to Akiyama Shun, who wrote *Nobunaga Hideyoshi Ieyasu*, noted that Nobunaga's victory was not all about the intelligence.[274] It was consequential, but not the sole reason in winning the battle. He mentioned the farmers; Buddhist and Shintō priests would have had a role in the outcome. He did bring up a pivotal point if Nobunaga lost the battle, the relationship with the Oda would have been over, and not overlooked.[275]

The people of Owari would have had to make a decision: stay with the Oda or the supposed Imagawa victors.[276] It could have changed the outcome of the battle. Two influential points about the people of Owari stated earlier. First, the people out of fear were helping Yoshimoto's troops during lunch. They did not know Nobunaga was coming with an army to kill Yoshimoto. Second, mistreating the people of Owari was not an option during his crusade. Mentioned earlier, if Yoshimoto was going to occupy Owari, he needed the masses and the land for future revenue. It was common during the Sengoku Era for farmers to work for their new lord if the previous one was disposed.

Continuing with Akiyama Shun's opinion on human intelligence, personally, I do not agree with him since prime intelligence is vital to winning battles and wars. The information Nobunaga received from Yanada Masatsuna was one of the key turning points in the battle. Without it, the possibility to spot Yoshimoto would have been slim. The Battle of Mikawa Kihara stated earlier (5 May 1560), was that engagement Nobunaga was looking for intelligence wise.

Naramoto Tatsuya had a different opinion. He had a column in his book, *Zusetsu Sengoku Bushō Omoshiro Jiten*, which explained the information was too important to ignore. In fact, the column mentioned Yanada's intelligence had more weight than Mōri Shinsuke taking Yoshimoto's head did.[277] Furthermore, compensated was Yanada because of his superb work. He received Kutsukake Castle and cash. In all honesty, he was paid more than Mōri Shinsuke and Hattori Koheita combined. For Nobunaga, intelligence was precious as gold. He was wise enough to use the data he received from Yanada Masatsuna at the right place and time. The tasks done by the three were significant, but not more important than the other was.

One more influential fact that intelligence was key. According to Owada Tetsuo's *Nobunaga Tettei Bunseki Jūnana Shō*, Yanada Masatsuna's intelligence was a major turning point in Sengoku warfare history. He pointed out that before the intelligence factor came in; it was all about military exploitation. That all changed at the Battle of Okehazama. He wrote in his book warfare went to the age of military exploitation to the age of intelligence.[278] The intelligence Nobunaga received made the element of surprise possible. Without it, Nobunaga would not have the chance to draw first blood.

Owada's statement about the new age of intelligence warfare confirmed it. Intelligence was one of Nobunaga's greatest assets throughout his military career and the Battle of Okehazama demonstrated it. The intelligence community would be full of envy today considering Nobunaga did not have nor would tolerate the bureaucratic chain of command.

Nobunaga's accomplishment with a small army was remarkable. Mentioned earlier in the book was Nobunaga's army before and after Okehazama. Jeroen Lamers's, *Japonius Tyrannus*, stated that Nobunaga's detachment was around 2,000 or 3,000 strong.[279] Also he somewhat agreed Nobunaga's forces was strong enough to deal with home province issues.[280] Whatever the case, his victory over Imagawa Yoshimoto was a stroke of military genius.

The small army Nobunaga used during the battle proved to be successful. Why Nobunaga's army was so triumphant? The answer was easy. If Nobunaga did have a larger force, the element of surprise would have been lost. A larger detachment would be easier to spot than a smaller one. Mitsuo Kure's opinion noted Nobunaga's intention was to slow down Yoshimoto's advance. Kure replied, "One or two minor victories over Yoshimoto would be enough to stop his advance on Owari..."[281] Even if Nobunaga were able to check him, it would not last long. Yoshimoto was too affectionate of Kyoto and would do anything to occupy the capital in his name. Nobunaga did not have the allied support Yoshimoto blessed with. He used his resources wisely and to the best of his knowledge.

Was Nobunaga's intention to slow down Yoshimoto's march and hold him off for awhile? The theory sounds cerebral enough, but he did not have the strength in numbers to hold off Yoshimoto for a lengthy campaign. On the other hand, Kure mentioned that Nobunaga was planning for a simple hit-and-run. If planned for a short time span; then, it could be reliable, but he did not have the logistics for a long and lengthy conflict. If he did have the numbers to hold the Imagawa advance, it might have been possible. A prolong guerrilla warfare was not an option.

Logistically speaking, Nobunaga had enough for a quick assault and that was all he had.[282]

What Kure failed to mention was that Nobunaga could not get any help from other allies. His alliance with the Saitō ended when Dōsan perished in 1556. If Dōsan was still alive during the time of Okehazama, the circumstances would have been different, and Nobunaga would have had the support from Mino just as he did in the Battle of Muraki in 1554. If that happened, Kure's opinion would have been valid and would have given Nobunaga other options besides a surprise attack. In the end, his only alternative was an ambush at Okehazama.[283]

The negative would be a smaller army had a much easier prospect to be defeated. The only probability to win the battle with a smaller detachment was a surprise attack. For example, the recent invasion of Iraq, the United States used a much lighter force. The lighter force allowed the military to advance quickly and completely surprise the Iraqi army. It was the same for Nobunaga. His small army was flexible enough to move rapidly on a moments notice. In conclusion, he had no other choice but to attack first and make the most of it.

Other examples would be battles that would occur later in the Sengoku Era. Engagements such as Kawanakajima 1561, Anegawa 1570, Mikatagahara 1572, Nagashino 1575, and Sekigahara 1600 had more complicated formations and planning had to be at its best. Nobunaga did not have the time, or the resources. The result: his small army was able to crush Yoshimoto's army at Okehazama.

Before Okehazama, Nobunaga defeated the Yamaguchi in 1552 at the Battle of Akatsuka. Moreover, his Oda rivals during the same year, the Battle of Kayatsu. He was outnumbered two to one and still triumphed. After Okehazama, he routed the Saitō at the Battle of Moribe in 1561. The Saitō force was larger than Nobunaga's (6,000) but was easily defeated. It proved Nobunaga's victory at Okehazama was no fluke with a small army (1,500). Most impressive about the victory was its quickness. The battle took place only days after Saitō Yoshitatsu passed away. He was shrewd to attack at a time when the Saitō were at their weakest. The same said for Imagawa Yoshimoto, overconfidence.

When Nobunaga defeated his rival brother Nobuyuki at the Battle of Inō in 1556, he was outnumbered again. His army was around 700, yet Nobuyuki had an army of 1,700 and still lost. The allied army received help from Hayashi Hidesada and Shibata Katsuie and nevertheless easily routed. The result would later cost Nobuyuki's life and the split in the Oda clan.

Still not convinced a smaller army can defeat a larger one. Akiyama Shun provided another prime lesson. He stated that Mōri Motonari's victory at the Battle of Itsukushima (an island southwest of Hiroshima) in 1555 was the naval account of Okehazama. Sue Harukata's fame to claim was he was loser of the ocean's version of Okehazama.[284] Motonari was fifty-nine years old when he won the Battle of Itsukushima. Take Akiyama's opinion seriously since it was a classic example of Okehazama without anything to do with Nobunaga. To win these kinds of battles tactics and patience played a vital role.

The Battle of Itsukushima itself depended on who controlled the strait. If that did not happened, cut off, the person who held the island. Stephen Turnbull noted in his book, *Samurai Warfare*, the success of the Mōri was to let the Sue capture the island, fortify the castle, and the fleet would be eventually be held up.[285] Rain played a pivotal function in the Mōri victory just as it did for Nobunaga at Okehazama.

Last, was Okehazama itself. Did Yoshimoto have to stop and have lunch? The common sense answer was no. He could have continued marching to Ōdaka or Narumi without rest. Stopping at Okehazama, all three things (rainstorm, Yanada's intelligence, and Nobunaga's small army) occurred and the deadly result was a superb victory by Nobunaga.

Okehazama's geography played a significant role for both men. The person who knew the geography had the advantage. The advantage clearly went to Nobunaga. The country boy learned the geography so well he was able to attack Yoshimoto with ease. Yoshimoto did not know the area and it cost him his life and the clan.

The battle not won by who had the most men and resources, but who had the best brains, prepared for battle, and use of the rare opportunities. Give credit to Nobunaga for making his gutsy plan to work. He knew the consequences, nevertheless further knew the spoils he would obtain if he had triumphed. From this time on, Nobunaga had a dream he sought just as other Sengoku daimyo and that was to unify the country under their own rule. Nobunaga's pace, speed, and mobility were dynamic. Okehazama proved he could bring an energetic army with short notice of time with total conquest.

His success was not an accident since planned well and his rivals were even in awe. Sengoku Japan had a new warlord to deal with. Nobunaga was young, energetic, power hungry, always thinking outside of the box, and the rare ability to use new tactics in crucial situations. Other Sengoku warlords had to think twice before dealing with Nobunaga from now on and in the future to come.

Post Okehazama

As for Yoshimoto's son Ujizane, he preferred the arts than war.[286] Sadler described Ujizane as "devoted to Japanese verse and football, and even more given up to drink and dalliance, and without any ideas about retrieving his position."[287] Ujizane had his father's weakness of alcohol, yet his father was a warrior and he mixed in his activities. In the end, he was nothing compared to father. The opulent and pacifist lifestyle of Ujizane would be the sole reason for the Imagawa demise.

When Yoshimoto left for the capital, his son was at the Imagawa Palace in Sunpu. A mistake that would cost the Imagawa clan considering it had the chance to retain Ieyasu as a potential future leader, but fumbled. The mistake was not Ujizane staying at Sunpu during his father's march to Kyoto, but his elitist lifestyle. Cannot stress enough how important the individual who is next in line must be capable of doing the job just as the previous one.

Why it was not a mistake to leave Ujizane home? The answer is simple. Ujizane stayed home because he was supposed to protect the home province. If Yoshimoto's march to the capital was lengthy, the Takeda and the Hōjō might have taken the opportunity to invade and catch Yoshimoto off guard. Even though the Imagawa, Takeda, and the Hōjō had a three-way peace pact, yet one had to cautious in case any of three families broke the truce.

Yoshimoto preferred the elitist aristocratic lifestyle similar to his son; however, he had more fighting spirit in him. As stated earlier most of the blame has to go to Yoshimoto himself. He had to know that his son was not fit for the job. If young Ieyasu was part of Yoshimoto's plan, then he was thinking wisely. However, he was unprepared for the tragic event. If Ujizane was somewhat compared to Nobunaga's son, Nobutada or Yoshimoto (just a little bit), the Imagawa clan might still have some political and military muscle, yet he was a farce and the clan went down hill quickly.

Yoshimoto's vassals after his death soon fled. For instance, the Ii were thinking of leaving out of dodge. The worst situation Ujizane wanted was his retainers leaving for greener pastures. He summoned the Ii to Sunpu for personal business and halfway there, Ii Naochika (Ii Naomasa's father), killed by Ujizane. It was a sign that conditions were awful for Ujizane and the Imagawa household. As for the Ii family, it was only common sense to team up with Ieyasu.

After the Oda-Tokugawa pact signed, Ieysau attacked his former partner Udono Nagateru. Nagateru, who was in command of Ōdaka Castle before Okehazama, was the new man in charge of Kaminojo. The assault was successful, and furthermore, his sons captured, and Nagateru killed. Ujizane still had Ieyasu's wife and children as hostages in Sunpu. Ieyasu would use Nagateru's sons as a bargaining chip in exchange for his wife and children. The task was accomplished quickly considering Ujizane would have Ieyasu's wife and children killed. As stated earlier, Ieyasu was a hostage himself and no doubt, the skills he learned from Sūfu helped. Ishikawa Kazumasa, a Tokugawa retainer, was the man responsible for the exchange.[288] For Ujizane, it was one more blunder and insult. It would only get worse for the Imagawa.

The year 1568, the Imagawa family fell apart. Yoshimoto's mother passed away and she was the glue that held the Imagawa clan after Yoshimoto's death. As an insult, Takeda Shingen of Kai invaded Sunpu. Ujizane would end up leaving Sunpu and retreated to Tokura Castle in Izu Province.[289] It was ironic one of Yoshimoto's old partners and one that enabled him an opening to occupy Kyoto would be the man who would destroy the Imagawa's role in Japan. As for Shingen, it was the perfect chance considering there was no love lost between the two clans. In short, it was business as usual in Sengoku Japan.

Nobunaga did meet Ujizane in 1575, almost fifteen years after the battle. Ujizane went to Kyoto to play kemari, a type of football game played by aristocrats. Nobunaga invited Ujizane to Shōkokuji in Kyoto on 20 March 1575, to play football.[290] Ujizane, the man who preferred the aristocratic lifestyle than war was now meeting at the time, the most powerful warlord in Sengoku Japan. Yoshimoto would have been joyful that his son was at the capital; however, it was for the wrong reason. Nobunaga had more military and political control in Japan than Yoshimoto or Ujizane could have ever imagined.

The Oda-Tokugawa Alliance

As for Nobunaga, the chance to have Ieyasu as an ally was powerful because now he could go to the capital without fear from the rear.[291] At first Ieyasu's advisers disapproved of the decision, but later it turned into a fruitful relationship that would benefit both parties. On 15 January 1562, the Tokugawa and Oda would become allies (Shokutoku Dōmei).

The alliance would last about twenty years and was a rare event during the Sengoku Era. The pact signed and a drinking party followed at Kiyosu Castle.[292] Ieyasu paid the visit and his respects to Nobunaga. In doing so made Nobunaga the senior leader of the alliance. The pact had benefits for the two. Nobunaga could now focus on the Saitō without worrying about Mikawa or Suruga. As for Ieyasu, he could now concentrate on unifying Mikawa. The Ikkō sect was not only a problem for Nobunaga, but for Ieyasu as well. Ieyasu was in debt to Nobunaga since he was a free man at last. If Nobunaga did not win the battle, Ieyasu would still have been in Yoshimoto's service.

Nobunaga treated Ieyasu with respect during the meeting. Even though the surrounding area of Kiyosu Castle was almost a mob due to the new visitors, he made sure everything went well.[293] He awarded swords to Ieyasu and Uemura Shinrokuro. To present Ieyasu a gift was normal during the Sengoku Era. He received two swords by various sword smiths. Nagamitsu made the long sword and the short sword by Yoshimitsu and Yukimitsu made Uemura's sword.[294]

The alliance strengthened even more with an arranged marriage between Nobunaga's oldest daughter and Ieyasu's son. Gotoku (Tokuhime) and Nobuyasu were married on 27 May 1567.[295] She was born in 1559 at Kiyosu Castle and only a year old when her father triumphed at Okehazama. Both were married at a very young age. Stability was always in jeopardy during the Sengoku Era, but both men knew if the alliance was going to succeed, marriage was necessary. Later Tokuhime would move to Okazaki Castle with her new husband. Since Nobunaga's daughter moved to Okazaki, it was Nobunaga who held the senior leadership of the alliance.[296]

As for the marriage it seemed everything was stable and until a letter sent from Tokuhime to Nobunaga. The letter would spell bad news for both Nobunaga and Ieyasu in 1579. Allegedly, it was Nobuyasu and Ieyasu's wife, Lady Tsukiyama (Imagawa Ujizane's cousin) was collaborating with the Takeda.[297] The situation was grave and Ieyasu did not fool around.

The word was out that Ieyasu's own house was about to erupt into chaos. He had no choice but to clean it up at once. He would do something that no man in the modern world would do: his son, Nobuyasu and his wife, Lady Tsukiyama received the death penalty! A decision that was not easy. If the situation went without punishment, the Tokugawa house could have been in a state of collapse along with the chance of a brake up of the Oda-Tokugawa alliance. The result was a wise one. Even though Ieyasu's wife and son dead, it meant that he still had control of his affairs at home. Ieyasu did not want to show Nobunaga he could not control his home affairs. As for Nobunaga, it proved he had senior leadership of the alliance and Ieyasu was still the junior partner. It would later prove the Oda-Tokugawa alliance was more important to stick together than to be apart.

One incident demonstrated the alliance was meaningful. For example, a rare event when Nobunaga present Ieyasu two bags of gold. Nobunaga was busy fighting other rivals and could not help Ieyasu fight the Takeda. In all honesty, Nobunaga wanted the Takeda wiped out just as much as Ieyasu wanted them destroyed.

In 1574, Takeda Katsuyori attacked and took over Takatenjin Castle.[298] Nobunaga and Nobutada did go out to relieve the stronghold, but they were too late. Nobunaga was not a happy man. He wanted to fight the Takeda, liquidate them, and did not have the opportunity to do it. If there was any threat to his Tenka, it was the Takeda clan. In return, he had to repay Ieyasu with two bags of gold mentioned above. Ieyasu was pleased with Nobunaga's gesture, yet at the same time, a little cloudy about the situation.

In the residence of Sakai Zaemon no Jō [Tadatsugu] two men brought out one leather bag for Ieyasu's inspection; noblemen and commoners, and high and low of [Ieyasu's] retainers admired this absolutely fantastic sight. They were all struck with amazement and said that they had never seen anything like this before. Everybody was impressed with Lord Nobunaga's might, but it was difficult to tell what was going on inside Lord Ieyasu's head.[299]

The movie *Kagemusha* did play out this episode. It showed Nobunaga presenting and explaining to Ieyasu he was sorry and was going to make it up. Ieyasu's retainers took the gold, yet he stood there in thinking about what just happened. He knew Nobunaga wanted to support him, but he had his own troubles to deal with. The alliance was the most important deed for the two men. *Kagemusha* did confirm quite accurately Nobunaga was the senior partner. At the same time, the movie revealed the two joking about foreign wine and the fall of the Takeda. Relationships had its good and bad times. Nobunaga and Ieyasu just went through the normal motions.

Conclusion

MODERN day military, the intelligence community, and politicians can learn from the Battle of Okehazama. It will remind the military how human intelligence can direct to demoralizing attacks, which can lead to victory. As for the intelligence community, everything matters and failure is not an option. Presidents, politicians, the military, and the like can learn from Yoshimoto's blunder: the successor is just as important as the current person in charge is. More important, never underestimate the enemy.

As for the CIA and FBI, intelligence is more powerful than the modern computer world. Computers and modern technology are important instruments, but can never replace human intelligence. For example, the hijackers of 9/11 used intelligence to outwit and outsmart the United States. It proved the United States government was weak in the intelligence department. It was by the stroke of God, the President of the United States did not end up like Yoshimoto in 1560. It does not take much to wipeout a large army or create chaos with intelligence and shrewd planning.

The United States military are slowly going back to the basics of hard, long, and dangerous work of gathering intelligence. A golden lesson learned from the encounter is not to be bureaucratic when it comes to intelligence. The main reason why Yanada Masatsuna was so successful was that he did not have any bureaucratic chain of command. Nobunaga hated delays. Key data cannot and shall not bog down. Hampered data causes confusion. Inform the highest in command. Second, is to hire people who have the Nobunaga character, leadership, do not listen to, reject political correctness, and have the drive to get the information at all costs no matter what the situation. Third, with the intelligence in hand, go on the offensive first never giving the enemy a break, destroying their morale, and kill the commander-in-chief soon as possible with no mercy.

Nobunaga was a master of intelligence considering he knew the stakes were high during his day. Life was cheap in Sengoku Japan and one had to do anything to survive. One must remember that there were no civil liberties in Sengoku Japan. Risky decisions were necessary and the norm. Rewarding a man of Yanada Masatsuna's caliber for informing where Yoshimoto was powerful. As stated earlier, Yanada changed Sengoku warfare forever. Military might is important; however, it is not necessarily the way to victory. Okehazama proved hard intelligence still is the way to victory or death.

In the future, the United States might to have to give up its own real estate as compensation. Money alone cannot buy intelligence or security. Nobunaga did both (money and land) and the result was instant success. It was a matter of life and death.

It is how the United States government and the military should treat intelligence. As a reward in the modern age, there are three: money, land, and tax exemptions (federal and state) for life. If Nobunaga were around today, an Okehazama event would never occur in the United States. He would have pushed his men to the brink for intelligence and kill enemy without mercy.

The question now would the CIA, FBI, the military, and politicians work with Nobunaga if he was around today? The answer is no. Too much bureaucracy, personal interests, and politics would cause Nobunaga problems. He would have given the CIA, FBI, and Homeland Security a run for their money. His energy and character alone would have given them the chills. Nobunaga would have given the intelligence community and the politicians a stern warning: do it my way or have your throat cut.

The modern day politician's picture would be bleak. Present day politicians are too timid, weak, and extremely politically correct now to tackle terrorism and evil government regimes. The reason is simple. The ACLU, United Nations, the media, activist judges, petty politicians, trial lawyers, and human secularists have too much power. Power they should never have in the first place. If the United States government tried to assassinate an Islamist terrorist leader there will be a huge outcry of human rights violation. Nobunaga would let them burn in hell! He was never feebleminded, did not have weak people in his circle, and never gave any civil liberties to his enemies. One must remember weak nations and people tend to perish rapidly.

What was the Nobunaga way? The way of Nobunaga: whatever it takes, no political correctness, does not give a damn what others think, and if possible, kill the enemy quickly. One has to remember why intelligence is too consequential to ignore, you, the military, and country not caught off guard. After the intelligence: strike first blood never giving the enemy a second chance!

Yoshimoto was an able leader of his clan, an administrator, a patron of the arts, a courtier, and a decent warrior. He had many weaknesses and the Imagawa house paid for it. He miscalculated Nobunaga's excellent use of intelligence, military genius, leadership, and character. The final story: never take the enemy lightly, pay attention to detail, and take the initiative first!

To wrap it up Sadler explains:

...Oke-hazama..., was one of the decisive actions of Japanese history, in that it placed Nobunaga in front rank of military leaders, and placed the acquisition of supreme power within his grasp.[300]

Sadler was right! Seven years later, he would occupy his former father-in-law's Mino domain. Along with the help of his Zen monk friend Takugen Shūon who created Nobunaga's famous slogan "Tenka Fubu." The slogan alone helped Nobunaga's goal to unify the country and it started with a miraculous conquest over Imagawa Yoshimoto on 19 May 1560. Stephen Turnbull agreed Nobunaga's victory at Okehazama was the starting point of the long process of unification. Better yet, fusion, which he used in his book, *War in Japan 1467-1615*.[301] The monk from Kyushu who went to Nobuhide's funeral in 1551 knew the fool was rare.

He was no idiot and was a remarkable self-made man from Owari with a mission: unify the nation as one!

Bibliography

Akita Hiroki. *Oda Nobunaga to Azuchi-jō*. Osaka: Sōgensha, 1990.

Akiyama Shun. *Nobunaga Hideyoshi Ieyasu*. Tokyo: Kōsandō Shuppan, 1997.

"The Battle of Okehazama." Toyoake City. <http:city.toyoake. aichi.jp/english/okehaza.html>

Berry, Mary Elizabeth. *Hideyoshi*. Harvard East Asian Monograph 146. 2nd ed. Cambridge (Mass.) and London: Council on East Asian Studies, Harvard University, 1989.

Brown, Delmer. "The Impact of Firearms on Japanese Warfare 1543-98," *Far Eastern Quarterly*. vol. 7, no. 3 (May 1948): pp. 236-253.

Cody, Billy J., Hyoe Murakami, and Thomas J. Harper ed., *Great Historical Figures of Japan*. "Unifiers of Japan Nobunaga, Hideyoshi, and Ieyasu," Tokyo: Japan Culture Institute, 1978.

Conlan, Thomas D. *Weapons & Fighting Techniques of the Samurai Warrior 1200-1877 A.D.* New York: Metro Books, 2008.

Cooper, Michael, SJ. *They Came to Japan: An Anthology of*

European Reports on Japan, 1543-1640. Berkeley: University of California Press, 1981.

Dening, Walter. *The Life of Toyotomi Hideyoshi.* 4 ed. Tokyo: The Hokuseido Press, 1955.

Fujimoto Masayuki. *Nobunaga no Sensō.* Tokyo: Kōdansha, 2003.

Hoff, Frank. "City and Country Song and the Performing Arts in the Sixteenth Century Japan." (ed) Elison, George. Smith, Bardwell. *Warlords, Artists, and Commoners Japan in the Sixteenth Century.* Hawaii: University of Hawaii Press, 1987.

Inoue Tsutomu. *Mō Hitosu Okehazama.* Tokyo: Kōdan Shuppan, 2000.

"Atsuta Jingu" *Jinja Kikō* Gakushū Kenkyū Sha. Tokyo: May 22, 2003.

Kaku Kōzō. *Nobunaga no Nazo.* Tokyo: Kōdansha, 2000.

----------. *Oda Nobunaga Zen Shigoto.* Tokyo: Fusosha, 2004.

Kōsaka Masataka and Sugimoto Sonoko. *Nobunaga no Senryaku.* Tokyo: Shogakukan, 1991.

Kure Mitsuo. *Samurai: An Illustrated History.* Boston: Tuttle, 2001.

Kusudo Yoshiaki. *Fūun Ji Nobunaga to Hiun no Onnatachi.* Tokyo: Gakushu Kenkyū Sha., 2002.

Lamers, Jeroen P. *Japonius Tyrannus.* Leiden: Hotei Publishing, 2000.

Lidin, Olof G. *Tanegashima: The Arrival of Europe in Japan.* Copenhagen: NIAS Press, 2002.

McMullin, Neil. *Buddhism and the State in Sixteenth-Cenury Japan.* Princeton: Princeton University Press, 1984.

Naramoto Tatsuya. *Zusetsu Sengoku Bushō Omoshiro Jiten.*

Tokyo: Mikasashobo, 1997.

----------. *Sengoku Bushō Monoshiri Jiten*. Tokyo: Shofu to Seikatsusha, 2000.

Nishigaya Yasuhiro. *Oda Nobunaga Jiten*. Tokyo: Tokyo do Shuppan, 2000.

----------. *Oda Nobunaga no Subete ga Wakaru Hon*. Tokyo: Shin Jinbutsu Ōraisha, 2002.

"Oda Nobunaga to Okehazama no Tatakai." *Bijuaru Nihon no Kassen*. No. 1, June 28, 2005.

Okada Masahito. *Oda Nobunaga Sōgō Jiten*. Tokyo: Yūsankaku, 1999.

Okamoto Ryōichi. *Oda Nobunaga no Subete*. 11 ed. Tokyo: Shin Jinbutsu Ōraisha, 2000.

Okanoya Shigezane. *Meishō Genkō Roku*. Tokyo: Nyūton Press, 1980.

Ōkubo Hikozaemon. *Mikawa Monogatari*. Translated by Kobayashi Takaaki. Tokyo: Nyūton Puresu, 1980.

Ōta Gyūichi. *Shinchō-Kō ki*. Translated by Sakakiyama Jun. Tokyo: Kōikusha, 1980.

Owada Tetsuo. *Imagawa Yoshimoto no Subete*. Tokyo: Shin Jinbutsu Ōraisha, 1994.

----------. *Rekishi no Documento: Okehazama no Tatakai*. Tokyo: Gakushu Kenkyū Sha, 2000.

----------. *Nobunaga Tettei Bunseki Jūnana Shō*. Nagoya: KTC Chūou, 2003.

----------. *Imagawa Yoshimoto*. Kyoto: Mineruboa Shobō, 2004.

----------. *Sengoku Gunshi no Kassen Jūtsu*. Tokyo: Shinchosha, 2007.

Oze Hoan. *Shinchōki*, ed. Kangōri Amane. 2 vols. Koten

Bunko 58 and 59. Tokyo: Gendai Shichōsha, 1981.

Rekishi Gunzō. "Sengoku Kassen Daizen." Tokyo: Gakken, 1997.

----------. "Gekishin Oda Nobunaga." Tokyo: Gakken, 2001.

----------. "Ninja to Nijutsu." Tokyo: Gakken, 2003.

----------. "Zusetsu Sengoku Chizuto." Tokyo: Gakken, 2003.

Sadler, A.L. *The Maker of Modern Japan.* London: Allen and Unwin, 1937.

Saigen Nihonshi. No. 49, April 23, 2002.

----------. No. 50, April 30, 2002.

Sato Hiroaki. *Legends of the Samurai.* Woodstock, New York: The Overlook, 1995.

Sengoku Bushō Retsuden. Besstau Takaurajimasha 604. August 31, 2001.

Shimura Kunihiro. *Nobunaga Senki.* Tokyo: Newton Press, 2003.

Soda Kōichi. *Jiten: Nobunaga wo Meguru 50 Jin.* Tokyo do Shuppan, 1991.

Solum, Terje and Rue K. Anders. *Saga of the Samurai Shingen in Command: The Takeda of Kai 4 (1549-1558).* Brookhurst Press, 2006.

Sugawara Makoto. "Heroes of the Unification of the Country," *The East* vol. XXIV, June 1988, pp. 45-51.

Sugimoto Sonoko and others, eds., "Okehazama no Tatakai," *Nobunaga no Senryaku.* Tokyo: Shogakukan, 1991.

Togawa Jun. *Kanzenseiwa Sengoku Kassen-shi.* Tokyo: Tachifū Shobō, 1999.

Totman, Conrad. *Tokugawa Ieyasu: Shogun.* San Francisco: Heian, 1983.

Tsumoto Yō. *Sengoku Bushō ni Manabu Jōhō Senryaku*. Tokyo: Kadokawa, 1995.

Tsunoda Ryūsaku, William T. deBary, and Donald Keene, eds., *Sources of Japanese Tradition*. vol. 1. New York: Columbia University Press, 1958.

Turnbull, Stephen. *Battles of the Samurai*. London: Cassel, 1987.

----------. *Samurai Warfare*. London: Arms and Armour Press, 1997.

----------. *War in Japan 1467-1615*. Great Britain: Osprey, 2002.

----------. *Japanese Warrior Monks AD 949-1603*. Great Britain: Osprey, 2003.

Varley, Paul H. *Samurai*. New York: Delacorte Press, 1970.

----------. "Oda Nobunaga, Guns, and Early Modern Warfare in Japan," James Baxter and Joshua Fogel (ed), *Writing Histories in Japan; Texts and Their Transformation from Ancient Times through the Meiji Era*, pp. 105-125. Tokyo: International Research for Japanese Studies, 2007.

Yoshikawa Eiji. *Taiko*. Translated by Scott Wilson. Tokyo: Kōdansha International Ltd, 1992.

Endnotes

1   Nishigaya Yasuhiro, *Oda Nobunaga no Subete ga Wakaru no Hon*, p. 85. For more information on the battle see Tsuge Hisayoshi, *Okehazama: Nobunaga no Shinbō Yoshimoto no Gosan* (Tokyo: PHP, 2004).

Chapter One

2   Walter Dening, *The Life of Toyotomi Hideyoshi*, pp. 90-91.

3   Nishigaya Yasuhiro, *Oda Nobunaga Jiten*, p. 114. See Akita Hiroki, *Oda Nobunaga to Azuchi-jō*, p. 3. *Rekishi Gunzō Shirizu*, "Gekishin Oda Nobunaga," p. 138.

4   Okada Masahito *Oda Nobunaga Sōgō Jiten*, p. 114.

5   Tsunoda Ryūsaku, William T. deBary, and Donald Keene, eds., *Sources of Japanese Tradition*, p. 303.

6   Jeroen Lamers, *Japanius Tyrannus*, p. 19. Modern name is now Ota-chō in Fukui Prefecture.

7   Ibid., p. 19. See http://odanobunaga.com for the complete Oda history in English. There is evidence that the Oda are offshoots of the Fujiwara family.

8   Ibid., p. 19.

9   Neil McMullin, *Buddhism and the State in Sixteenth Century Japan*,

p. 59. Nobuhide belong to the Oda Kiyosu branch. The (Yamato) Kiyosu branch consisted of three families: Oda Inaba no Kami, Oda Tozaemon, and Oda Danjō no Chū. Nobuhide belonged to the Oda Danjō no Jō. The other main Oda branch was the (Ise) Iwakura.

10   Ōta Gyūichi, *Shinchō-Kō ki*, Introductory Book, section 1. (Hereafter: intro: 1ect.), p. 44.

11   Mary Elizabeth Berry, *Hideyoshi*, p. 35. See Lamers, p. 46. Lamers listed the 1530s and 1540s for Nobuhide's expansion into Mikawa.

12   Ibid., p. 35. See Lamers, p. 46. Lamers mentioned that when Ieyasu was a child, he was captured by the Toda and delivered to the Oda in 1547.

13   Sugawara Makoto, "Heroes of the Unification of the Country," *The East* Vol XXIV, June, pp. 45-51.

14   Ibid., pp. 45-46.

15   Delmer Brown, "The Impact of Firearms on Japanese Warfare, 1543-98," *Far Eastern Quarterly* vol. 7 (May 1948), p. 238. See Olof G. Lidin, *Tanegashima*, p. 146. Nobunaga used guns at the Battle of Okehazama.

16   Okanoya Shigezane, *Meishō Genkō Roku*, p. 244.

17   McMullin, p. 90.

18   Sugawara, p. 46.

19   McMullin, p. 90.

20   Gyūichi, Introduction: 1, p. 45.

21   Ibid., p. 45.

22   Ibid., Introduction: 3, p. 47.

23   Ibid., p. 47.

24   It is debatable of Nobuhide's death. Some books recorded as saying his death occurred in 1549. See Gyūichi, Introduction: 9, p. 54. It stated Nobuhide's death in 1549. Nobunaga would have been sixteen years old if his father died in 1549.

25 Sugawara, p. 46.

26 McMullin, p. 90.

27 Gyūichi, Introduction: 9, p. 55.

28 Lamers, p. 24.

29 Okanoya, p. 287.

30 *Rekishi Gunzō*,"Gekishin Oda Nobunaga," p. 86.

31 Sugawara, p. 46.

32 Gyūichi, Introduction: 7, p. 51.

33 For a biography of Saitō Dōsan see Dobashi Jijū, *Saitō Dōsan* (Tokyo: Seibidō, 1997).

34 *Rekishi Gunzō Shrizu* 50 "Sengoku Daizen," p. 58.

35 Berry, p. 35.

36 Paul Varley, *Samurai*, p. 103.

37 *Saigen Rekishi.* No. 49 April 23 2002, p. 9.

38 Gyūichi, Introduction: 10, pp. 56-59.

39 Ibid., pp. 56-59.

40 Ibid., p. 56-59.

41 *Rekishi Gunzō*,"Gekishin Oda Nobunaga," p. 18.

42 Gyūichi, Introduction: 10, pp. 56-59.

43 Ibid., pp. 56-59.

44 Ibid., p. Introduction: 17, p. 73.

45 Lamers, p. 26.

46   Gyūichi, Introduction: 17, p. 72.

47   Ibid., p. 73.

48   Billy Cody, "Unifiers of Japan Nobunaga Hideyoshi, and Ieyasu," *Great Historical Figures of Japan*, p. 156.

49   Ibid., p. 157.

50   Ibid., p. 157. Nobunaga stabbed Nobuyuki to death.

51   McMullin, p. 84.

52   Cody, p. 157. Battle of Iwakura took place in 1559.

53   Ibid., p. 161.

54   Gyūichi, Introduction: 34, p. 117.

55   Ibid., p. 117.

56   Ibid., pp. 117-118.

57   Ibid., p. 118.

58   Ibid., p. 118.

59   Ibid., p. 118.

60   Ibid., p. 118.

61   Gyūichi, Introduction: 26, pp. 101-102.

Chapter Two

62   Stephen Turnbull, *Battles of the Samurai*, p. 34. Tokugawa Ieyasu was born in 1542. He was the son of Matsudaira Hirotada.

63   Gyūichi, Introduction: 2, p. 46. See Tsutomo Inoue, *Mō Hitosu no Okehazama*, p. 26. It has a list of early conflicts between the Oda and Imagawa.

64   Okada, p. 307.

65   Ōkubo Hikozaemon, *Mikawa Monogatari*, pp. 139-140.

66   Lamers, p. 46. See Owada Tetsuo, *Okehazama no Tatakai*, p. 56.

67   Gyūichi, Introduction: 16, p. 68.

68   Ibid., p. 69.

69   Ibid., p. 69.

70   Ibid., p. 69.

71   Ibid., p. 70.

72   Ibid., p. 71.

73   Ibid., p. 71.

74   A.L. Sadler, *Maker of Modern Japan*, p. 51. See Owada Tetsuo, *Okehazama no Tatakai*, pp. 104-105. Owada stated that Ieyasu attacked Terabe (Toyota-shi, Terabe-chō) and Suzuki Hyūga no Kami Shigetoki in the Second Month 1558.

75   Ibid., p. 51.

76   Ōkubo, Chapter 2, p. 154.

77   Sadler, p. 51. See Turnbull, *Battles of the Samurai*, p. 36.

78   Ibid., p. 51.

79   Ibid., p. 51.

80   Owada, *Okehazama no Tatakai*, pp. 50-51. See Okada, *Nobunaga Sōgō Jiten*, pp. 217-218.

81   Okada, p. 319. See p. 316 for a minor battle against the Imagawa in 1556 and known as the Battle of Noderahara in Mikawa.

82   Ibid., p. 319.

83   Lamers, p. 29.

84   Berry, p. 9.

85   Ibid., pp. 8-9. Hideyoshi's father Yaemon, served under Oda Nobuhide as a musket-carrying grunt.

Chapter Three

86   Sugawara, p. 47.

87   Berry, p. 36.

88   Ibid., p. 36.

89   Naramoto Tatsuya, *Sengoku Bushō Monoshiri Jiten*, p. 232.

90   Berry, p. 27.

91   Sadler, p. 48.

92   Ibid., p. 48.

93   Ibid., p. 48.

94   Owada Tetsuo, *Imagawa Yoshimoto*, p. 217.

95   George Elison, "Introduction: Japan in the Sixteenth Century," *Warlords, Artists, and Commoners Japan in the Sixteenth Century*, pp. 2-3.

96   Ibid., p. 3.

97   Berry, p. 27.

98   Ibid., p. 27.

99   Owada, *Okehazama no Tatakai*, p. 37. Yoshimoto has been labeled as the tenth, eleventh, or twelfth in line for the Imagawa house.

100   Ibid., pp. 38-39.

101   Yoshimoto's earlier name Baigakushōhō?

102   Owada, *Imagawa Yoshimoto*, p. 127.

103   Sadler, p. 48.

104   *Rekishi Gunzō*, "Sengoku Kassen Daizen," pp. 64, 74.

105   Owada, *Imagawa Yoshimoto*, p. 50.

106   Sadler, p. 48.

107   Berry, p. 34.

108   Ibid., p. 33.

109   Ibid., p. 37.

110   Sadler, p. 48.

111   *Saigen Nihonshi*. April 23 2002, pp. 24-25.

112   Ibid., p. 24. See Terje Solum, Anders K. Rue, *Saga of the Samurai Shingen in Command: The Kai of Takeda 4 (1549-1558)*, p. 48.

Chapter Four

113   Sugawara, p. 47.

114   Gyūichi, Introduction: 24, p. 91.

115   Lamers, p. 58.

116   Owada Tetsuo, Okamoto Ryōichi, "Nobunaga no Senryaku," *Oda Nobunaga no Subete*, p. 100.

117   Ibid., p. 100.

118   Kure Mitsuo, *Samurai: An Illustrated History*, p. 142.

119   Owada, *Imagawa Yoshimoto*, pp. 240-241.

120   Okada, p. 306.

121   Owada Tetsuo, *Imagawa Yoshimoto no Subete*, pp. 30-31.

122   For a different view of the battle see Hamada Akio, *Okehazama no Tatakai: Kagetora no Kakusaku to Nobunaga no Sakuryaku* (Tokyo: Toyo Shuppan, 2007).

123   Owada, *Okehazama no Tatakai*, pp. 10-12. Probably Yoshimoto's army left two days earlier than the main army. It allowed the vanguard to clear any hostilities along the way. It is now accepted that Yoshimoto departed on 12 May.

124   Ibid., p. 43.

125   Ibid., p. 43.

126   Ibid., pp. 16-20, 42.

127   Ibid., p. 86-87.

128   Ibid., p. 87. Other lesser known Oda forts include Mukaiyama, Shōkōji, and Hikamiyama.

129   Sadler, p. 52.

130   Ibid., p. 52.

131   Sugawara, p. 49.

132   Stephen Turnbull, *Samurai Warfare*, p. 18.

133   Conrad Totman, *Tokugawa Ieyasu*, p. 31.

134   Lamers, p. 46.

135   Ibid., p. 46.

136   Turnbull, *Samurai Warfare*, p. 18.

137   Ōkubo, Chapter 2, pp. 153-154.

138   Gyūichi, Introduction: 24, p. 90.

139   Owada, *Okehazama no Tatakai*, pp. 95-97.

140   *Sengoku Bushō Retsuden.* Bessatsu Takarajimasha 604. August 31 2001, pp. 50-51. See Hashiba Akira, *Hattori Hanzō to Kage no Ichizoku* (Tokyo: Gakken, 2006).

141   Owada, *Okehazama no Tatakai*, pp. 47, 110-111.

142   Ibid., p. 106-107.

143   Ibid., p. 107.

144   Turnbull, *Battles of the Samurai*, p. 37.

145   First general killed by a matchlock rifle?

146   Owada, *Okehazama no Tatakai*, p. 110.

147   Sadler, p. 53. See Owada, *Okehazama no Tatakai*, pp. 113-114. The book listed the number of troops by both armies on the day of the battle. Gyūichi, Introduction: 24, p. 93. Yasuyoshi died in 1557 and his son, Yasutomo led the army.

148   Owada, *Okehazama no Tatakai*, pp. 113-114.

149   Sugawara, p. 47.

Chapter Five

150   Kaku Kōzō, *Nobunaga no Nazo*, p. 448.

151   John Whitney Hall, "Japan's Sixteenth Century Revolution," *Warlords, Artists, and Commoners Japan in the Sixteenth Century*, p. 10.

152   Gyūichi, Introduction: 24, p. 90. See Paul Varley "Oda Nobunaga, Guns, and Early Modern Warfare in Japan," p. 114. He has a theory that Nobunaga played the fool because he was worried about spies.

153   Owada, *Okehazama no Tatakai*, p. 91. Hayashi Hidesada banished from the clan in 1580.

154   Yoshikawa Eiji, *Taiko*, p. 190.

155   Owada, *Okehazama no Tatakai*, p. 93.

156   Sadler, p. 54

157   Kusudo Yoshiaki, *Fūunji Nobunaga to Hiun no Onnatachi*, p. 70. See *Owada, Okehazama no Tatakai*, p. 124. It mentioned that one of Nobunaga's pages held the hand drum.

158   Ibid., p. 70. See Yoshikawa, *Taiko*, p. 195.

159   Frank Hoff, "City and Country Songs and the Performing Arts in the Sixteenth Century Japan," *Warlords, Artists, and Commoners Japan in the Sixteenth Century*, p. 138. For more information on *Atsumori,* see "Oda Nobunaga to Okehazama no Tatakai," *Bijuaru Nihon no Kassen* No. 1 (June 28 2005), pp. 20-21.

160   Owada, *Okehazama no Tatakai*, p. 125.

161   Gyūichi, Introduction: 24, p. 90.

162   Sugimoto Sonoko and others, eds., "Okehazama no Tatakai," *Nobunaga no Senryaku*, p. 127. Sugimoto noted that Nobunaga also ate victory chestnuts and kombu. Nobunaga loved strong flavored country foods.

163   Yoshikawa, p. 195. Whether it was true or not "Tsukinowa" was the name of the horse and Nobunaga was quite fond of horses.

164   Sugimoto, p. 127.

165   Gyūichi, Introduction: 24, pp. 90-91.

166   Inoue, p. 228. See Oze Hoan, *Shinchōki*, p. 59.

167   Owada, *Okehazama no Tatakai*, pp. 128-129.

168   Ibid., p. 133.

169   Yoshikawa, p. 197.

170   Soda Kōichi, *Jiten Oda Nobunaga wo Meguru 50 Hito*, p. 278.

171   Sadler, p. 54.

172   Ibid., p. 54.

173   Ibid., p. 54.

174   Ibid., p. 54.

175   Owada, *Okehazama no Tatakai*, p. 134.

176   Ibid., p. 136.

177   Ibid., p. 138. It was constructed with mud, lime, and grease.

178   Ibid., p. 172.

179   Ibid., p. 173.

180   Sadler, p. 55.

181   Owada, *Okehazama no Tatakai*, p. 144.

182   Nishigaya, p. 130.

183   Lamers, p. 26.

184   McMullin, p. 84.

185   Owada, *Okehazama no Tatakai*, p. 149.

186   Ibid., 144-145.

187   Gyūichi, Introduction: 24, p. 92.

188   Inoue, p. 122.

189   Sato Hiroaki, *Legends of the Samurai*, p. 235.

190   Owada, *Okehazama no Tatakai*, pp. 160-161.

191   Yoshikawa, p. 205.

192   Ibid., p. 205.

193   Owada, *Okehazama no Tatakai*, pp. 160-161.

194   Ibid., p. 195. *Rekishi Gunzō* "Ketteiban Zusetsu Sengoku

Chizucho," p. 115.

195   Ibid., p. 195.

196   Ibid., p. 195.

Chapter Six

197   Ibid., p. 195. See Naramoto Tatsuya, *Sengoku Bushō Monoshiri*, p. 85. See Okada, p. 287.

198   Sugimoto, pp. 129-130.

199   Owada, *Okehazama no Tatakai*, p. 156. See Gyūichi, Introduction: 24, pp. 92-93.

200   Ibid., p. 155.

201   Owada, *Imagawa Yoshimoto*, p. 222.

202   Ibid., p. 222.

203   Sadler, p. 55. See Thomas D. Conlan, *Weapons & Fighting Techniques of the Samurai Warrior 1200-1877 A.D.*, p. 138. Conlan mentioned that Uesugi Kenshin fortified temporary lodgings or camps. However, Yoshimoto's camp was not fortified.

204   Yoshikawa, p. 206.

205   Sadler, p. 55.

206   Gyūichi, Introduction: 24, p. 94.

207   Turnbull, *Battles of the Samurai*, p. 38.

208   Owada, *Okehazama no Tatakai*, p. 190. See *Saigen Nihonshi* No. 49, April 23 2002, p. 36. Owada also has an article that explained one of Nobunaga's gunpaisha might have predicted the storm. Also Owada, *Sengoku Gunshi no Kassen Jūtsu*, pp. 116-117.

209   Ibid., p. 190.

210   Sato, p. 236. See Gyūichi, Introduction: 24, p. 93.

211   Gyūichi, Introduction: 24, pp. 93-94.

Chapter Seven

212   Sugawara, p. 48.

213   Gyūichi, Introduction: 24, p. 94.

214   Owada, *Okehazama no Tatakai*, p. 197.

215   Owada, *Imagawa Yoshimoto*, pp. 239-240.

216   215 Owada, *Okehazama no Tatakai*, p. 197.

217   Inoue, p. 184.

218   Owada, *Okehazama no Tatakai*, p. 196.

219   Gyūichi, Introduction: 24, p. 94.

220   Owada, *Okehazama no Tatakai*, p. 198.

221   Yoshikawa, p. 207.

222   Ibid., p. 211.

223   Gyūichi, Introduction: 24, p. 95.

224   Sugimoto, pp. 132-133.

225   Owada, *Okehazama no Tatakai*, pp. 199, 206.

226   Ibid., p. 207.

227   Ibid., pp. 209-210. The *Okehazama Kassenki* is an Edo war chronicle.

228   Ibid., p. 210.

229   Yoshikawa, p. 214.

230   Owada, *Okehazama no Tatakai*, p. 216. The numbers differ from

document to document. The number of decapitated heads taken in battle was approximately, 3,000.

231   Ibid., p. 216.

232   Ibid., p. 214. See Thomas D. Conlan, *Weapons & Fighting Techniques of the Samurai Warrior 1200-1877 A.D.*, p. 116. The sword engraved "The sword of Imagawa Yoshimoto, who was careless and killed by Nobunaga on 19.5.1560."

233   Ibid., p. 219.

234   Turnbull, *Battles of the Samurai*, p. 38.

235   Naramoto, *Sengoku Bushō Monoshiri Jiten,* p. 82.

236   Owada, *Okehazama no Tatakai*, pp. 205-206.

237   Inoue, pp. 189-190. See http://www.city.toyoake.aichi. jp/english/okehaza.html. According to Shimura Kunihiro's, *Nobunaga Senki*, the landmark (Senninzuka) built for the soldiers who fought at Okehazama. pp. 216-217.

238   Gyūichi, Introduction: 20, p. 84.

239   Sugawara, pp. 48-49.

240   Owada, *Okehazama no Tatakai*, p. 224.

241   Ibid., pp. 222-223. There is a possibility that some of the Imagawa army left Chiryū with 5,000 soldiers to attack Kariya and Ogawa.

242   Ibid., p. 222.

243   Dening, pp. 106-107. Hideyoshi, "Though Yoshimoto is dead, he has a son living and there is no saying that his retainers may not come against us a second time unless something is done to prevent it."

244   Owada, *Okehazama no Tatakai*, p. 225. Tenpakuji had some relationship with Yoshimoto's deity, but abandoned during Meiji Era.

245   Ibid., pp. 224-225.

246   Ibid., p. 225.

247   Gyūichi, Introduction: 24, p. 98.

248   *Saigen Nihonshi*, p. 39.

249   Owada, *Okehazama no Tatakai*, p. 203.

250   Turnbull, *Battles of the Samurai*, pp. 39-40.

251   Owada, *Okehazama no Tatakai*, p. 203.

252   Ibid., p. 203.

253   Togawa Jun, *Kanazenseiwa Sengoku Kassen-shi*, p. 46.

Chapter Eight

254   Kaku Kōzō, *Oda Nobunaga Zen Shigoto*, p. 121.

255   Sadler, p. 56.

256   Ibid., p. 56. In 1575, Mizuno Nobumoto forced to commit suicide for selling supplies to the Takeda.

257   Owada, *Okehazama no Tatakai*, p. 232.

258   Stephen Turnbull, *Japanese Warrior Monks AD 949-1603*, p. 47.

259   Ōkubo, p. 161.

260   Sugawara, p. 48.

261   Sadler, p. 50.

262   Kure, p. 144.

263   Sadler, p. 49.

264   Owada, *Okehazama no Tatakai*, p. 37.

265   Turnbull, *Battles of the Samurai*, p. 39.

266   Yoshikawa, p. 209.

267   Ibid., p. 204.

268   Owada, *Imagawa Yoshimoto*, p. 240.

269   Sadler, p. 48.

270   Owada, *Okehazama no Tatakai*, p. 16.

271   Ibid., p. 14-16. See *Saigen Nihonshi* April 30 2002, p. 38.

272   Berry, p. 34.

273   Sugimoto, p. 139.

274   Akiyama Shun, *Nobunaga Hideyoshi Ieyasu*, p. 37.

275   Ibid., p. 37.

276   Ibid., p. 37.

277   Naramoto Tatsuya, *Zusetsu Sengoku Bushō Omoshiro Jiten*, p. 177.

278   Owada Tetsuo, *Nobunaga Tettei Bunseki Jūnana Shō*, p. 40.

279   Lamers, p. 29.

280   Ibid., p. 30.

281   Kure, p. 144. See Paul Varley, "Oda Nobunaga, Guns, and Early Modern Warfare in Japan," p. 114. Fujimoto Masayuki stated that there is no evidence to prove Nobunaga's attack was a surprise. Fujimoto never mentioned oral history and oral history unfortunately left out these days due to inconsistencies. The evidence gathered and the battlefields visited, Nobunaga had no choice but to use a surprise attack on the Imagawa camp. Also Fujimoto Masayuki, *Okehazama: Nobunaga no Kishū Shinwa wa Uso datta* (Tokyo: Yōsensha, 2008).

282   Tsumoto Yō, *Sengoku Bushō ni Manabu Jōhō Senryaku*, pp. 47-49. Victory was due to guerrilla warfare.

283   Varley, "Oda Nobunaga, Guns, and Early Modern Warfare in Japan," p. 114. Varley mentioned that Nobunaga did not use the surprise attack tactic for rest of his military career. Varley also stated that the Japanese military leaders knew the importance of the Battle of Okehazama and used it during Pearl Harbor in 1941. See Fujimoto Masayuki, *Nobunaga no Sensō*, pp. 91-99, 110-111. Highly detailed, but disagreed with his theory.

284   Akiyama, p. 34-35.

285   Turnbull, *Samurai Warfare*, p. 101.

286   Sadler, p. 57.

287   Ibid., p. 57.

288   Totman, p. 33.

289   Owada, *Okehazama no Tatakai*, p. 224.

290   Ibid., p. 247. See Salder, p. 74. Ieyasu wanted to give Ujizane some of his old domain, Suruga back. Nobunaga smartly refused the request.

291   Sadler, p. 57.

292   Owada, *Okehazama no Tatakai*, p. 250.

293   Sadler, p. 58.

294   Ibid., p. 58.

295   Okada, p. 171.

296   Lamers, p. 48.

297   Ibid., p. 51. (Princess Sena) Lady Tsukiyama was selfish and wicked. She was Imagawa Yoshimoto's niece and her father was Sekiguchi Ujihiro (Yoshihiro).

298   Ibid., p. 51.

299   Ibid., p. 51.

Conclusion

300   Sadler, p. 56.

301   Stephen Turnbull, *War in Japan 1467-1516*, p. 40.

Acknowledgements

Firstly, would like to thank the Lord who has given me strength (John 3:16). Without him, I could not finish this project. Mr. Brent Massey, my publisher, thank you for everything! To my parents and grandparents who have helped me. Thanks! Many thanks to Professor Matsuda Yukitoshi formerly taught at Gifu University. Without his wisdom, would have failed. He taught everything about Nobunaga when I was studying at the University of Gifu 2000-1. God Bless him! Many thanks to the staff at the Gifu City Museum of History; they played a vital role in my personal interests in Oda Nobunaga. Kitsuno and Obenjo of Samurai Archives thanks a million. You guys rock! To my former professor at SDSU Owen Griffiths who taught Japanese History at San Diego State University. He had no choice but to put up with my Nobunaga facts. To the Birlew Family who helped financially with my trips to Japan. Mrs. Ikuko "Iku" Jackson. Thanks for the translations. Mr. Naoki Okumura. You are the man! Oda Nobunaga freaks, Tenka Fubu: "Rule the Empire by Military Force!" Ms. Kaoru Hirao, you will always be my little Nōhime. May God bless you always and forever!

About the Author

Les Paterson graduated from San Diego State University in 2003 with a bachelor's degree in history. Education includes one year at Gifu University 2000-1 and the Japanese tea ceremony (Urasenke School). At Gifu University, he studied Japanese and the career of Oda Nobunaga. He enjoys traveling to Japan, cooking, soccer, church, and the study of Oda Nobunaga. You can contact the author at his webpage at http://otsuke.blogspot.com for questions and comments.

www.ingramcontent.com/pod-product-compliance
Lightning Source LLC
Chambersburg PA
CBHW032103080426
42733CB00006B/391